T0294135

THE
HARD
YARDS

Highs and Lows
of a Life in Cricket

THE
HARD
YARDS

Highs and Lows
of a Life in Cricket

MIKE YARDY

First published by Pitch Publishing, 2016

Pitch Publishing
A2 Yeoman Gate
Yeoman Way
Worthing
Sussex
BN13 3QZ
www.pitchpublishing.co.uk

ISBN 978-1-78531-156-7

Typesetting and origination by Pitch Publishing
Printed by Bell & Bain, Glasgow, Scotland

Contents

Acknowledgements

BRUCE TALBOT, who collaborated with Mike Yardy on this book, and Mike would like to thank John Barnett for his help in checking the completed text. Images were sourced from Mike's family collection and Phil Barnes, of the Sussex CCC library.

Foreword
by Matt Prior

I WAS 12 years old when I first encountered Mike Yardy. There was I, not long having arrived from South Africa playing age-group cricket for the Sussex under-12s. In the age group above there were a number of players who already had a reputation for being good enough to go all the way and Yards was one of them. I was in awe of the guy. He was *the* name in Sussex age-group cricket at the time and everyone you spoke to thought he would go on and have a career in the game. They were right, and what a career it's been.

We played the majority of our youth cricket together and slowly worked our way through the ranks until we both finally broke into the Sussex first team a few years later. I always respected Yards for the player he was but there was a game in 2001 when I decided that there was one characteristic in his game that I wanted to emulate. We were playing Somerset on a bit of a green top at Hove. It was only my first year on the staff and I hadn't faced too many really quick bowlers. That day Somerset's Richard Johnson – fighting for England recognition – really hit a rhythm and came charging down the slope. The dressing room was nervous, the ball was flying around everywhere off the pitch and batting was just horrible! Yards was different however. He didn't seem affected, and if he was you couldn't tell. He fought tooth and nail that morning and while wickets were falling at the other end he wasn't to be moved. He played and missed, he took blows, he got sledged but all of this only seemed to spur the second-year professional on. He was doing what he did his whole career. Fight!

He fought for every inch that day and that was a trait that remained with him his whole career. He scored 73 (not his best score by a mile) but it stands out to me as one of the best innings I ever saw him play and an innings that had a huge effect on my own game and mentality as well. That day I decided that's how I wanted to be too. I was going to give everything I had to being a professional cricketer and commit fully to my team. I was going to fight.

Yards always committed everything he had to improve, he was always looking to make himself better. Changing the fundamentals in terms of the way you bat and then, a few months later, doing the same with your bowling was a brave decision at the time but it massively paid off for him. Within a couple of years Yards was an England cricketer and although we didn't play together too often for our country it was always an even more special time for me when Yards was alongside. Two Sussex school boys living the dream we always spoke about.

Yards will be the first to admit that there have probably been more talented cricketers than him during his 16 years in the game but how many could say with total honesty that they achieved as much or made the absolute utmost of their ability as he did? In my team I would always have the player that gets the most out of himself than one that promises the world and delivers nothing. At the 2010 Twenty20 World Cup he played a massive part in England's success. During so many of the games he and Graeme Swann applied the pressure during the important middle overs with his left-arm spin. He was a vital cog in the England wheel and, as his friend, I was so proud of what he achieved when England lifted the trophy. Only 11 England cricketers have ever won an ICC World Cup and Michael Yardy is one of them.

In 2009 he realised another dream and became Sussex captain. Yards is Sussex born and bred and no man would have felt more honoured to lead the county than him. He's always been a student of the game and had a very shrewd tactical brain. In T20 in particular he had this knack of second-guessing what the opposition were going to do next. Sometimes it was just a hunch, but more often than not it worked and when he was performing well with the ball, as he did that year when Sussex won finals day at Edgbaston, there were few better leaders in the country than him. As a leader he embraced the ideals and team ethos which Peter Moores had first instilled at Sussex when we both came onto the staff. Yards always held those values we had close to his heart and continued to do so right up until 2015 when he retired.

Admitting he was suffering from mental illness was an incredibly brave decision. To decide that you're not fit enough to keep playing for your country is very, very tough, as I found out myself a few years later. Although we were always close and spoke often, particularly on that tour, it was only after England had played Ireland in the 2011 World Cup that I realised just how serious his problems were. It was heart-breaking to watch Mike go through what he did. He felt all alone and could no longer cope. Hearing Mike describing so honestly after that Ireland game just how lonely he'd become and the battles he was fighting, there was only one thing to do. I know how difficult his decision to come home and get treatment was to make but it was 100% the right one. It's a struggle he is always going to have to face, but five years on Mike knows how to deal with it and, of course, he has the fantastic support of Karin and their family which I know has been invaluable to Yards over the years.

Leaving the game for good can be very difficult to accept for any professional sportsman but Yards was fortunate to be able to retire from the game in 2015 on his own terms. Filling the gaping hole in your life which was once occupied with playing sport for a living can be difficult but I know how much he enjoys studying a subject which has always interested him. I know too that Mike will do everything to make himself the best sports psychologist he can. His own personal experience will make him exceptional at this I am sure and I don't doubt that he will be a huge asset to his fellow professionals one day.

Life moves on quickly and it already seems an age ago that Yards and I were playing professional cricket together at the ground we both grew up at and loved. We were both hugely fortunate to play in such a successful era for both Sussex and England and I look forward to reminiscing about them all one day, maybe on a bike! What do you think, Yards?

Introduction

PUTTING together this book has really made me appreciate the number of people who have helped me through my life so far, during the good times and the bad. I would love to mention everyone but that would probably need a book of its own. However, I'm sure they know who they are and how much I appreciate all that they have done for me.

I would like to thank my parents, Howard and Bev, for their unbelievable support when I was a little boy wondering if could turn my dream of playing cricket for Sussex into a reality.

Sussex County Cricket Club have played such a big part in my story so far. Actually, it is people that make an organisation special, not the name. All the people who worked at the club during the 16 years I was player and captain helped to make it such a special time for me.

The coaches and players at both Battle and Hastings Priory Cricket Club, for teaching me early in my cricketing journey all about the values of being a team player.

Thanks to all the wonderful team-mates I had the opportunity to play with and learn from, for both Sussex and England, and for all the unbelievable support and friendships gained.

And the friends who have supported me whether I was doing well or badly and took the mickey accordingly!

To Bruce Talbot, who has followed my career from the very start, thanks for all your hard work in turning my waffling anecdotes into a book I am very proud of.

Lastly, to Karin and the kids. I'm not one for big gestures but suffice to say you are all amazing and I'm so proud of what we have achieved together.

You have taught me that spending time as a family means so much more than the day to day stuff. It has not been an easy ride for us but we have always faced the challenges head on.

Enjoy my story.

Mike Yardy
Brighton, April 2016

1

Breakdown

ANDY Flower knew the signs. I'd spoken to the England head coach when I first left the squad during the one-day series against Pakistan in September 2010. The morning I literally couldn't get out of my hotel bed in Southampton. The morning I was staring at the ceiling and felt like the walls were closing in.

"Look, you'll know when I'm in trouble. Just look into my eyes."

Seven months later we were in Colombo, preparing for the World Cup quarter-final against Sri Lanka. It should have been one of the highlights of my career. Instead, I remember standing in front of the mirror in my hotel room wishing I could pull my own face off and be someone else. I didn't want to be Mike Yardy anymore.

A few hours later and we were practising under the floodlights. Well, the other players were. I was just going through the motions. A zombie. I felt like my head was in a cloud and I couldn't find my way out.

No one in the England management team knew me better than Mushtaq Ahmed. We'd been Sussex team-mates for six years and when he joined the England set-up I worked with him regularly on both my bowling and batting. He was a friend as well, someone I could confide in.

He came over. I must have looked terrible, that same haunted expression I'd been staring at for the last few days in the mirror of my hotel room.

"Yards, go home."

That's all. Not that he needed to say anything else. He knew. I knew.

My first thought was one of overwhelming relief because someone had recognised I was struggling and, more importantly, was making a decision for me. I wouldn't have to confess how I really felt to anyone. Not to Mushy, Andy Flower or Matt Prior, my Sussex team-mate who must have worn out the carpet in the hotel corridor traipsing from his room to mine to make sure I was okay.

Okay? I wasn't okay. But I couldn't tell Matt. That's the thing with depression. You become a great actor. You're trained to RADA standard when it comes to putting on a brave face.

I went to see Andy. He was brilliant, as he had been since he sent me home from Southampton a few months earlier and then put me in touch with Brett Morrissey, a psychologist I'd seen several times since and who was always on the end of the phone when I needed someone to try and explain to me why I was feeling the way I did. Why everything – not just cricket – had become such an effort.

Andy's priority was to get me out of India as soon as possible, not just for my sake of course but to make sure my sudden departure wasn't a huge distraction for the team with such a big game coming up. That was fine by me. The last thing I wanted was to have to look any of my team-mates in the eye and admit I had let them down. That I had let my country down.

They smuggled me out the next morning. The team doctor accompanied me to the airport and the ECB made sure someone was waiting at Dubai Airport (where we had a stop-over before continuing to London) who could take me into the first-class lounge for a couple of hours.

I knew the ECB would have to issue a statement. I told them I was quite happy if it explained that I was coming home to seek treatment for depression. If they had asked me to feign an injury so they could get a replacement for me in the squad I'd have gone along with that, but they had checked the regulations with the ICC. As well as groin strains, dodgy knees and broken fingers, the diagnosis of a mental illness is a good enough reason for a team to call up reinforcements.

Sitting in the lounge in Dubai Airport. My phone starts bleeping, then again, and again and again and again for what must have been 15 minutes. Text message alerts. The news was out. I phoned Karin and explained what had happened and that I was on my way home. She was in tears. Later she told me it was because she was worried about the impact that the treatment I would need might have on our families and friends.

She had to tell them, which cannot have been easy. Outside a very small circle of people, they had no idea of the problems I was experiencing.

Our two young children, Syenna and Raffy, were oblivious of course. They would be thrilled to see me earlier than expected when I came back from the World Cup and would be dragging me off to the swings and the park as soon as I'd put my bags down. They were too young to understand why I kept having to go away for long stretches and they certainly didn't realise that for the past couple of years, and on more than one occasion, going off to represent my country was the last thing I wanted to do.

I must have received a hundred texts when I was sitting in Dubai Airport. That was nice and everyone was genuinely concerned but the ones I wanted to receive more than any were from my England team-mates. I felt I had let them down and the only way I would feel even slightly better about my situation would be to read some supportive messages from them.

Kevin Pietersen was first, the others followed. Thank God for that. All I felt as I read them was an overwhelming sense of relief. I just needed that reassurance, that they didn't feel bad about me for leaving the World Cup.

The statement the ECB had put out in conjunction with my county, Sussex, was now on the internet. Looking back, I'm not sure if I was in the right place mentally to make such a snap decision on what it said. But at the time I felt 'why should I be judged?'

I knew the truth would come out at some stage. There was no point in hiding from it any longer. I'd been living a lie for so long about the extent of my issues, although it would be another year before the penny finally dropped and I realised my illness wasn't actually related to cricket.

It was related to me.

2

In denial

FOR the first two years of my England career I had treated it as something to relish and enjoy. I knew, in my heart of hearts, that I was never going to have that long in international cricket and, although I was playing well for Sussex at the time, when I was called up for the first time in August 2006 it was still a very pleasant surprise. I decided to make the most of every moment.

A few weeks after I made my debut in a T20 international in Bristol against Pakistan I was named as England A captain for a tour to Bangladesh. It was a strong squad. Eight future international players were in the group and, just after we got back, having won the Test series 1-0 and the one-day matches 2-1, our coach, Peter Moores, replaced Duncan Fletcher in the main England role. Not many England captains win on the subcontinent and I enjoyed leading the side. Peter must have given me a good report to Mark Robinson, my coach at Sussex, because when we got back I was made Chris Adams' vice-captain and knew that when Grizzly eventually retired I would almost certainly be his replacement.

Peter probably knew he was favourite to succeed Fletcher at some point and that he might be working with quite a few of us who went to Bangladesh further down the line. I knew from his time at Hove that he was a hard taskmaster who demanded very high standards and we were all desperate to do well for him. My own personal performances in Bangladesh were nothing to write home about but I enjoyed the tour and felt I had led the team well.

Over the next 18 months I only played three more games for England, all in a home series against West Indies – two T20s and a one-day international in 2007. I was told I was still on the selectors' radar and in 2008 I was named captain of England Lions, which was the new name for the A team, for a tour to India. To try and battle-harden us a bit more in subcontinental conditions, Peter Moores had arranged for us to play in the Indian domestic four-day competition, the Duleep Trophy. David Parsons was the coach this time and we got on fine.

On the pitch I did well. In the two Trophy games we played I was top scorer. Against West Zone in Vadodara I made 169, having earlier scored 57 in the second innings of our first match against Central Zone. We didn't reach the final but a few guys who went on to have long and fulfilling England careers, including Jonathan Trott and Monty

Panesar, established their credentials with their performances on that tour, although Monty had already played for England by then.

I'm still extremely proud of the way I handled myself and the mental strength I showed during those two months in India. To perform as well as I did when I felt as bad as I did for most of it would rank as one of the highlights of my career because if someone had told me at any stage during that trip that I could go home, I'd have been off like a shot.

Mornings were the worst. Because of the time difference, it was too early to call Karin back at home so if there was the opportunity to train at the ground, or go to the gym, I'd be there every day without fail. The others must have thought that, as captain, I was trying to set the right example when all I was doing was trying to take my mind off this awful black feeling I had. Everything – and I mean everything – was a struggle, even simple things like getting up in the morning or having a couple of beers with the other players.

Of course I know now that I was in complete denial about depression. I didn't confide in anyone about how I really felt. Actually, to be more accurate, I didn't want to confide in anyone. I spoke to the medical staff at the ECB and while it was good to talk and try and explain that I didn't feel 'right' I made the decision that I would have to plough on. Stiff upper lip and all that. And in any case, what did 'right' feel like?

So I put on that brave face again.

The only person I could really confide in was, of course, Karin. She spent most of nearly every conversation we had whilst I was in India trying to talk me out of quitting the tour. Even if I had, I doubt if I would have been able to confess what was really wrong with me, as I did when I left the World Cup squad three years later, even to the person closest to me. She was worried about the long-term ramifications for my England career. If I pulled out that would probably be it for me and international cricket. It was a sobering thought.

While others on the tour kicked on with England in 2008 I wasn't chosen for any of the internationals that summer – the home series against New Zealand or South Africa. That was fair enough but there was a Lions series that year which I wasn't considered for. No one knew how much of a struggle the Lions tour had been for me mentally, but I felt I had some credit after batting so well in India.

Also, I thought that my performances in some of the white-ball cricket I played for Sussex – we won the Pro40 one-day league that year – deserved to be recognised, even if it was for the Lions. There was no feedback, no one spoke to me to say why I wasn't in the mix.

Everything was hard work during that summer of 2008. I enjoyed the vice-captaincy at Sussex but even socialising with my team-mates, when we won a trophy or an important match, was a bind. I knew something was wrong but, once again, I ignored it. I remember walking out to bat against Hampshire in a Championship match at Arundel in July in tears. My opening partner, Chris Nash, was completely oblivious to my state of mind. My senses were so scrambled that I ran myself out for 12.

Why was I feeling like this?

Eventually I spoke to Sussex coach Mark Robinson. Of course I didn't tell him how I really felt but he was very sympathetic and gave me a few days off and that seemed to help. At the same time, I was given a book called *A Lifetime on Lessons and Leaders* by a successful American basketball coach called John Wooden. That helped me re-evaluate a few things as well and, briefly at least, eased my mind a little bit.

Our second child Raffy was born in August 2008 and a few days later we decided to go to Australia for the winter. Most professional cricketers do that at the start of their careers so it felt a bit strange to be making the trip as a 28-year-old with my wife and two young children in tow. Of course we went for the right reasons. Warm weather and good, competitive cricket to keep me ticking over but it soon became a nightmare entirely of my own making.

The club had found us a house in a place called Lathlain which wasn't quite as nice as we had expected. Within a couple of days of arriving I became paranoid that the house would be broken into. It got so bad that I would wait for Karin and the kids to fall asleep before undertaking my own lengthy nightly security check, which involved making sure every window was locked and ramming chairs and tables against bolted doors, like I was barricading myself in for a shoot-out in a Wild West saloon.

It was the first manifestation of what I now know is a form of OCD when I would be engulfed by intrusive thoughts. If you had been burgled, you would go through your reactions logically. You would phone the police, get the insurance company in to assess the damage and determine what had been stolen. Then you would change the locks.

I went to extreme lengths. I used to scan the local newspapers to see if a crime had been committed in Lathlain and if a burglary was reported on the TV news I convinced myself we would be next. I would spend hours reading up on the crime statistics in Perth. The only way you could have convinced me that we weren't going to get broken into and robbed blind would have been to show me something that said the crime rate in the area we were staying was 0%. Even then, I doubt if it would have made any difference to my state of mind.

Finally, on New Year's Day 2009, I'd had enough.

The logical thing to do was to seek specialist help. This wasn't normal behaviour was it? My response was to decide there and then, as 2008 became 2009 and I sat bolt-upright in bed, that we were going to move. With two young children, and living in a city we didn't really know, that was quite an upheaval but move we did. There were still occasional moments when I thought we were going to be the next local crime victims but we settled into a better house in a nicer area and those feelings gradually subsided.

I enjoyed the cricket and played well in what was a very good standard. I was proud of how I did considering that for most of my waking hours I thought that in the middle of the night intruders were going to break in and I'd have to confront them.

A few months later and back in Sussex for 2009 I began my first season as captain. I was still ignorant about the state of my mental health; I continued to believe I would be able to cope with any distractions or those invasive feelings that things were getting on top of me.

It helped, of course, that we had a really successful season, winning two trophies and getting to the one-day final at Lord's against Hampshire. I had lots to occupy my mind. This was a good thing.

Physically and mentally the summer was tough though. Two of the pillars of Sussex's successful decade, Chris Adams and Mushtaq Ahmed, had retired and the senior players had to perform, day in day out, if we were to be successful. Your preparation could be the worst ever but if you went onto the field and performed then it was fine. And we did. It was the most enjoyable season of my career, topped off with a return to India for the first ever competition between winners of the various T20 competitions around the world. That went okay. By the time we got back I was physically knackered but otherwise things seemed to be under control. Captaincy brought extra responsibilities and being busy took my mind off things.

My form in the domestic T20 that summer had got me back into the England reckoning and I was named in the initial 30-man squad for the 2010 World Cup in the Caribbean. That gave me a focus for the winter of 2009/10. I wanted to be as fit as I could should I get into the final squad so I trained like a maniac, twice a day most days.

I did get selected and when we met up before heading off to the West Indies I sat down with Andy Flower, who had succeeded Peter Moores as coach. I told him that I was at my best when I was busy. I needed to be active. I'd already spoken to a psychologist and left the consultation feeling very positive. Having not played for England for three years, I regarded taking part in the World Cup as a one-off, not the re-birth of my international career. I was really looking forward to another opportunity.

And we won it, which was brilliant because it was so unexpected, and I enjoyed the celebrations which followed as much as any of my team-mates. After the success in 2009 with Sussex and now this I was riding the crest of a wave.

Then it all started again.

My solid performances in the World Cup persuaded Andy and the selectors that I deserved another chance in 50-over cricket. England were preparing for the 2011 World Cup and the feeling was that in India and Sri Lanka, who were co-hosting the tournament, England should go with two spinners, myself and Graeme Swann. Left-armer and off-spinner.

I played in the first home series of the 2010 summer against Australia and did okay but whenever the opportunity presented itself after a match I would go home because that's where I felt most at ease. We clinched the series at Old Trafford and there were still a few stragglers leaving the stands and walking out of the ground when I was driving out of the car park to head back to Sussex. I wasn't the only player who headed for home between matches when the opportunity arose, but I don't think anyone was doing so on such a regular basis. I know the guys I played with for England appreciated the role I performed in the team and that they respected me as a cricketer. Not at the time of course, but only when it was all over for me with England less than a year later. It was the illness which made me feel that I didn't quite belong, whereas at the World Cup a few months earlier I had felt totally engaged in the England set-up.

Things started building up again. Pressure inside my head.

Between England games there were Sussex commitments. We played Hampshire in a T20 game at the Ageas Bowl and Murray Goodwin ran me out – not deliberately of course, it was just one of those incidents which happen now and again, especially in that format. A mix-up, a good throw and I was gone.

But in my mind Murray had done it deliberately. As I set off for the pavilion he turned his back on me, probably because he was embarrassed. I turned around and laid into him.

"What the fuck are you doing?"

"Why the fuck did you do that?"

The Hampshire players and the umpires couldn't believe what they were seeing. I was that close to walking back and confronting Murray. I don't know what stopped me to be honest. I was playing well at the time. A couple of days earlier I'd made 76 not out against Essex at Hove in another T20 when, for the first time, I felt like an England player going back to play county cricket and feeling I was too good for that standard. Graham Gooch, who was coaching Essex, told Mushy that it was good to see England players returning to domestic cricket and looking like they were dominating at that level.

Not that I was thinking too much about that when I got back to the changing room. Murray was fuming when he returned, which I totally understood, and the next day I apologised to him in front of the rest of the squad. It was something I had never done before and was totally out of character, an incident which I regretted the moment it happened. Murray was an unbelievably good team man and a great help to me during good times and bad. Why did I turn on him?

It was another warning but once again I chose to ignore it. The apology was made and we moved on but a few weeks later I was struggling again.

We were playing Pakistan in a one-day series and I was in the squad. Great news.

If only.

When I received the call-up the first thing I thought was 'I don't want to go and play for England.'

Battles were raging inside my head. I kept trying to convince myself it would be fine. "You've worked hard all your career for opportunities like this – you could be going to another World Cup. What's wrong with you? Keep busy, work hard. You'll be fine."

I remember playing with the kids in the park on the day I had to drive to Cardiff to meet up with the squad for the first of two T20s. It was too late by then, unless I feigned an injury. Karin talked me round in the end and all I kept saying to myself as I headed down the M4 was, "You can't let people down." Over and over and over again, until I got to the hotel.

And when I got there everything was fine.

I was man of the match in the first T20 international for the first time in my England career after taking 1 for 21 and scoring an unbeaten 35. The next day my four overs went for just ten and I hit the winning runs for the second game in a row as we clinched the series 2-0.

I should have been happy. Deep down I wasn't.

But I did what I'd always done. Default mode. I knuckled down and got on with it.

I was chosen for the one-day games and did okay. I picked up a couple of wickets at Durham and then got us over the line with 13 not out at Headingley where our victory clinched the series.

There was a party to celebrate but I didn't go, I preferred to be at home. It's a big regret of mine that at the time my illness stopped me enjoying all the elements of playing for England. I wish I could wind the clock back. I always enjoyed a celebration after a win with a few beers but at this point my mood was pretty low. I wasn't allowing myself to enjoy the party.

I have so much admiration for someone like Paul Collingwood. He loved the England experience – every single element of it: travel, train, play, socialise. I don't think it's a coincidence that he had such a fantastic international career because of that. He represented his country 300 times during an eight-year career and during that time there were probably more naturally gifted players whom he kept out of the team. He was a captain's dream because he never gave up and his team-mates loved him. Colly was always up for it. Even when he got nought, dropped a catch or his bowling was smashed around the park he would just accept that he'd been outperformed by a better opponent, which of course tended to happen a lot at the highest level.

By the time we got to The Oval I just wanted it to be over.

I didn't bowl that badly – 1 for 42 off eight overs – but Umar Gul gave me a bit of a working-over with the ball before he had me leg before for four. We lost the game and Pakistan celebrated wildly. It was their first win since the spot-fixing story had broken at Lord's a few weeks earlier.

My figures were okay but I wasn't bowling well. The pitches were flat and Pakistan's batsmen, with all their experience of dry, turning pitches, played spinners relatively easily. I was struggling to accept that on occasion someone would get the better of me. Don't get me wrong, when I did take a wicket or play a good shot I loved it. It was afterwards, when I started over-analysing everything, that I struggled to cope.

I knew I had some serious issues but still I refused to be proactive. At that stage, if someone had told me I was suffering from depression I would probably have not believed them. I didn't go around with a permanent frown on my face. I wasn't miserable all the time. How could I be depressed? I felt bad sometimes but I just got on with it. As you do. I always felt worse when I was on my own, but my moods were such that all I wanted to do was be alone.

I certainly didn't feel I could talk about my feelings to any of my England team-mates. Matt Prior had more than an inkling that something wasn't right and another good friend in the dressing room at the time was Ian Bell. Ian and I did a lot together when we were on England duty. We would hit the gym, perhaps have a meal in the evening and even the odd drink or two. But we'd mainly talk about cricket. I could never imagine having a discussion with Matt, Ian or anyone else, apart from Karin, about mental health and how I really felt.

At Lord's I went wicketless and made just nine runs as Pakistan levelled the series with one game to play. I didn't feel I was contributing anymore. I just needed someone to tell me exactly that so I could quietly move out of the spotlight.

I wanted to give up international cricket there and then.

At the hotel the following morning I met Andy Flower for breakfast. He was great, once again.

He assured me that, despite struggling against Pakistan, he still saw me as an important member of the 50-over squad heading into the 2011 World Cup. I felt a bit better, but not much. I certainly didn't feel I could tell Andy how I felt mentally.

Before the series finale at Southampton Andrew Strauss, the captain, told me I wouldn't be playing. They were going to play an extra seamer because they didn't think the pitch would spin at all.

I wasn't even going to play but the following morning, I could not get out of bed. I didn't want to face anyone or do anything. All I wanted to do was go home. I phoned Karin in floods of tears. She tried to reassure me, to comfort me but it wasn't making much difference this time. Somehow I managed to drag myself to Andy's hotel room. I must have looked like a ghost when I knocked on his door. Andy was just about to leave for the ground and after hours of trying to find the courage to confess to him how I felt the words came tumbling out.

For weeks all this had been building up inside me.

I broke down in front of the England coach. Weeks, months, probably years of pent-up feelings came pouring out.

Andy was once again brilliant in the way he handled the situation.

I left the hotel and drove home. The fact I hadn't been selected could easily be explained. There was no reason to tell anyone – the rest of the team or the media – why I wasn't there as the series came to an end.

Back at home I felt better. Andy phoned me every day for the next few days and put me in touch with a sports psychologist he knew called Brett Morrissey. Brett phoned me, came down to the house and we met regularly for the next few weeks, often in London at the offices of a friend of his who was a solicitor. I cannot explain the sense of relief I felt, for the first time, to be able to speak to someone who could break down and explain, in fairly simplistic terms, why I felt the way I did in certain situations. I was wary of going on any medication and although I eventually did I can't say with any certainty that it made any difference to how I felt or dealt with certain situations.

I started to take small steps towards understanding my illness and how to deal with it. I tried different things to help me understand, including keeping a journal so I could write down my feelings on a daily basis. Over the next few weeks and months I started to feel a bit better. Being at home certainly helped.

With all that in mind, my decision to fly to the other side of the world and spend Christmas in New Zealand, playing in their domestic T20 tournament for Central Districts, might seem daft. It even involved spending Christmas on my own. Karin did come out for a week or so in December 2010 but flew back to be with the kids for the holidays. We had a game on Boxing Day so we flew down to Wellington on Christmas Eve and on Christmas Day I trained with the squad, went for a run and then had lunch in Nando's. I have been abroad for Christmas quite a few times and it never feels like Christmas anyway when you're in another country. It was just a normal day to me.

It was a big risk being away from home for so long, a test if you like. But I handled it okay. Of course I missed the kids opening their presents and stuff like that but if I ever felt bad I could ring Brett. I learned subsequently of course that someone suffering from mental illness doesn't get better in the same way you might recover from a cold but I began to feel good about myself and, for the first time in a while, I was looking forward to meeting up with the England lads when I flew to Australia for the T20 and ODI series at the start of 2011.

England had just regained the Ashes and the players who were due to stay on for the one-day series were dropping like flies. There must have been about 25 of us when we began with two T20s in Adelaide, but we split the series 1-1 and I played well. I got both David Warner and Shane Watson out after they'd smashed us all over the park, including hitting Graeme Swann's first three balls for six. Two nights later in Melbourne I took 2 for 19 and got Warner and David Hussey out this time in front of a massive crowd.

That first game, which we eventually won by one wicket, was a fantastic occasion under the lights in front of another full house. Before I arrived in Australia I made a promise to myself to try and embrace each game as much as I could, to play as if it was the last time I'd be pulling on an England shirt and it was a good time to be playing for my country. The victory in Adelaide secured a record for the most consecutive T20 wins and the buzz around the squad, on the back of the Ashes triumph, was tremendous.

We all needed to keep a smile on our faces when the one-day series started. Australia were very strong and thrashed us 6-1 – they clearly had something to prove to themselves after the Ashes defeat. I played in six of the games and didn't pull up any trees although I did make my career-best at Perth when I scored 60 not out.

But despite having a modest one-day series I left Australia feeling pretty good. I'd done very well in the T20s and the fact

I had played in nearly all of the ODIs suggested Andy and the selectors saw me as a likely pick for the World Cup after I was named in the squad.

Looking back now, returning home before flying out to India for the start of the tournament was a big mistake. I should have gone straight to India from Australia and cracked on because I was in that cycle of train, rest and play. I might have been okay. I think I could have managed.

Instead, we came home for just four days, which is no time really because you need a couple of days to get over the jet lag. It was great to see Karin and the kids again but as soon as I got to Heathrow to meet up with the rest of the squad, I could sense those familiar feelings closing in on me again: anxiety, self-doubt, uncertainty. But, unlike Southampton a few months earlier, I didn't want to succumb. Despite being thrashed by the Australians we genuinely felt we had a chance of winning the World Cup. If someone had tapped me on the shoulder at the airport gate and told me I didn't need to get on the aeroplane I would have ignored them.

It was a World Cup.

"Come on, you can do this."

We played a couple of warm-up games against Canada and Pakistan and I did okay but the selectors decided to go with just one spinner against the Netherlands in our first match in the competition proper in Nagpur.

Swann took 2 for 35 and was our best bowler as they scored 292 and we got home with eight balls to spare. We needed to play two spinners.

We moved on to Bangalore to play India and I made my World Cup 50-over debut. It was a fantastic experience playing in front of 38,000 passionate fans and the game was a real cliff-hanger. Chasing 339 to win, we needed 14 off the last over and ended up scoring 13 so it was a tie. Bowling to their big stars – Yuvraj Singh, Sachin Tendulkar and the rest – on their own patch was an unforgettable experience. I bowled the last six overs at one end which was pressure I'd never experienced before but I got Yuvraj out just when he was threatening to do some serious damage.

MS Dhoni hit one ball back at me during my spell so hard that I thought I had broken my finger. When we started our run chase I was watching it in the hospital consulting room while they checked me over before returning to the ground with nothing more than bad bruising.

So I settled into a daily routine of training, resting and playing which I thought I could cope with, but by the time we played Ireland a few days later, also in Bangalore, everything was starting to become hard work again. Losing the game, and in the way we did after scoring 327 on a wicket that did a bit, was unforgivable really and the dressing room was a pretty desolate place afterwards. All we could hear was hundreds of celebrating Irishmen.

I went back to my hotel room and burst into tears.

I should have done something there and then. Rung Brett, got him to call Andy and tell him I couldn't continue. Of course I should have done that. But that would have been showing weakness again. That would have meant letting

Andy and the players down. In a World Cup. No, I couldn't do that. I had to crack on again. So I did.

I had even greater responsibility in Chennai four days later. I opened the bowling against South Africa and ended up taking 1 for 46 from nine overs. We won a thrilling game by six runs and were back on track for the quarter-finals, but I knew the selectors wouldn't put up with my lack of a meaningful contribution with the bat for too much longer. I was struggling to score runs at a decent tempo on the slow pitches.

I was dropped for the next game against Bangladesh in Chittagong, which we lost by two wickets. Now, without the security of knowing that I was in the team, I got more and more down. Hours between training sessions spent in the hotel room, the only interruption Matt Prior knocking on the door.

"You okay mate?"

"Yes, don't worry about me."

We beat West Indies in our final group game to scrape into the knockout stages but it was another nine days before the quarter-final against Sri Lanka in Colombo, five of which we'd be spending in Delhi waiting to find out where we'd be playing our next match. With nothing to focus on apart from cricket I just felt and looked worse and worse. There would be brief moments of happiness when I phoned home and heard Karin's reassuring voice at the end of the line.

But it couldn't go on.

A knock on the door. "Andy, I can't do this anymore. I've got to go home."

3

Baby steps

I STILL wonder why I felt, after a few days back at home, that things would soon be back to normal.

The reality was I knew that my England career was probably over. During the following few months of 2011 I would see Geoff Miller, the chairman of selectors, on the county circuit quite often and he would always reassure me that 'the door is still open'.

But being out of the England picture was a good thing, surely? That's what I kept telling myself in the weeks after I came back from the World Cup. Playing for England had made me depressed. I wasn't in that environment anymore. I was free to concentrate on playing for Sussex. Without that added pressure of trying to sustain an international career I convinced myself I'd be fine. I'd be at home, with the family. I'd have that comfort blanket around me.

When the plane touched down at Heathrow I wasn't sure what to expect. I hoped that there would be no TV cameras and interviewers at the arrivals gate and, fortunately, there weren't any. The ECB had asked the media to give me some space and they had. Good. I can slip back home, have a few days with Karin and the kids getting back to normal, receive some more help from Brett Morrissey and then return to cricket with Sussex.

No chance.

Karin picked me up and told me that her Facebook account had been hacked by a national newspaper. The ECB had requested that the media leave me alone but Karin had been harassed with messages on her private page all day. I was having a small taste of what celebrities go through on a daily basis and it was the last thing I needed. Why can't you just leave us alone?

Once I was back at home and the front door was shut I felt a lot better.

I deliberately avoided the sports channels on TV because I knew they would be talking about me. What I didn't expect when I turned on the local news in the evening was to see a reporter outside the County Ground discussing depression with a so-called expert they had found from somewhere. They might have been a specialist in mental illness, but they weren't a specialist in me.

It was the same the next day, but this time they had a bit more to discuss. Geoffrey Boycott had been on *Test Match Special* back at the World Cup and been asked about my sudden departure from the squad. I couldn't believe what I was hearing.

"I'm very surprised, but he must have been reading my comments about his bowling. That must have upset him because it's obviously too much for him at this level.

"If there's any blame attached it's partly to the selectors who have done an excellent job on picking the Ashes side but I'm sorry, he's not good enough at this level. He doesn't bowl for Sussex in their Championship matches, he bowls in the one-day, but at this level, sorry, bowling round-arm, into the legs, without any spin and without any flight, you've got to be so perfectly accurate.

"I'm sorry, on good pitches, you're not going to hold good players down and if it turns, he doesn't have a quality enough action to get them out. For me, he was always going to be a liability or a poor choice at international level out here."

It was only a couple of days later, when it was pointed out to him on *Test Match Special* the reason why I had come home early, that he backed down. He had been crass and insensitive but his views, although stridently expressed, were not unusual and I soon realised that his appraisal of my situation was one I was going to encounter again and again over the next few weeks and months in some form or another.

Another TV reporter on the local news had found a spokesman for a mental health charity to condemn Boycott's comments and he was very supportive, but this was not the reaction I expected the statement I had made in the first place to generate. I certainly didn't want the intrusion.

For a couple of weeks at least, I wanted to be left alone with Karin and the kids but I knew I couldn't become a recluse. Three or four days after I got back we went for a stroll on the Brighton seafront. Looking back, it was probably one of the most conspicuous places I could have gone. Saturday afternoon, end of March with better weather on its way. Lots of people about, some of whom would no doubt have recognised me. I kept my head down, but I was aware that people were looking at me. The last thing I wanted was some sort of celebrity status. People staring. I wasn't comfortable until we were safely back at home and the door was shut again.

Brett and I met up again a few days later. For the next few weeks we'd get together on a weekly basis with him commuting to London from his base in Birmingham and me from Sussex. Before the first session I genuinely thought that once I'd spoken to him I would soon feel better again. I was out of the England bubble. That's what had made me ill, hadn't it? But during the first two years of my captaincy of Sussex there had been a lot of bad days too, which I'd covered up. We'd won trophies, we'd been successful. I'd been successful. But still I felt I hadn't performed as well as I could. Still I'd felt I was letting people down.

Brett was very supportive. We'd sit and chat for a couple of hours and when I left those initial sessions I felt elated. Then, a few hours later, reality would kick in. It was great to speak to someone who was so understanding but his underlying message was clear. This was something I'd have to cope with for the rest of my life. It wasn't to do with England. It wasn't to do with Sussex. It wasn't to do with cricket. It was me. Mike Yardy, a sufferer of depression.

I knew that if I had other things to occupy me it would help. I wanted to resume my Sussex career as soon as I could, but Brett warned me that I wouldn't be able to go back to Hove and just pick up the threads like I was coming back from a groin strain or a sore knee.

"Baby steps Mike, baby steps."

A lot of people at Sussex were not fully aware of my situation. Most knew what everyone else did, that I was being treated for depression. As I prepared to go back to the County Ground about a fortnight after coming home I actually found it quite amusing imagining what sort of reaction I'd get from the other players when I turned up again.

One of the lads broke the ice. "Christ Yards – where did you get those?" he asked, pointing at my socks as we got ready for training. Everyone in the room pissed themselves laughing.

I quickly realised that the other lads picked up on my mood. Look, I didn't walk around permanently with a face like a wet weekend. I was just trying to be my normal self, even though I wasn't sure what 'normal' was anymore. I could sense their awkwardness around me so I tried to remain as upbeat as I could. All the usual dressing-room stuff, talking about football, what we'd watched on TV, or taking the piss out of each other's clothes. If I was okay then I felt so were the others. Gradually I began to feel a bit better. It was good to be back in the team environment, working in the nets, feeling bat on ball again, getting a good sweat on in the gym. Thinking at the end of each day that I'd achieved something.

Baby steps. Brett was right.

There was absolutely no pressure on me from Mark Robinson, the Sussex coach, or anyone else to play again. I was told to take as much time as I wanted. Murray Goodwin captained the team for the first two Championship matches. We lost the opening game against Lancashire at Liverpool and then beat Durham.

I knew I wasn't ready to go away with the team yet for any length of time but I felt ready to play. Our first Clydesdale Bank 40-over home game of the season was against the Netherlands on Bank Holiday Monday, 2 May. That would be my comeback. I wasn't named in the squad which was announced the day before to avoid any unwanted publicity but I captained the team and performed quite well, taking 1 for 36 from my eight overs and then scoring 39 off 52 balls on a slow early-season pitch to help us to our first win of the tournament. I enjoyed it and during the game I felt absolutely fine. It was very low key, just 1,742 people watching and a couple of journalists in the press box, both of whom knew that I wouldn't be prepared to speak about things after the game, and thankfully respected that.

A couple of days later we were due to start a Championship game at the Rose Bowl against Hampshire. We were living in North Lancing at the time so it was a fairly easy commute for me. I spent a couple of days with the squad, practising in the nets and generally being part of things again and I was able go home every night. All very low key again, just how I wanted it to be.

Our next four-day match was against the champions Nottinghamshire at Hove. I felt good and wanted to play. My only concern was that it was being shown live on Sky Sports. If anything did go wrong it would all be very public and that was the last thing I needed. Sussex told Sky beforehand that I wasn't going to do any interviews and, once again, I wasn't named in the matchday squad. There were a few more journalists in the press box but, again, they gave me some space which I appreciated.

Nottinghamshire had a strong team out, including Stuart Broad, and the re-laid wicket was quite lively but we outplayed them and won by nine wickets with a day to spare. I made 22 in our first innings and although I felt like I was scratching around a bit I just put it down to my lack of exposure to the red ball. Other than that there were no issues. So far, so good.

We had two more Championship games at Hove before the end of May. We beat Somerset by eight wickets and then drew with Yorkshire despite making them follow on for the first time in 31 matches. My own contributions were fairly modest: a solitary run against Somerset and run out for 16 in the Yorkshire match but there were no problems in either game. I thought I was getting better.

It was now time for the Twenty20 group stages and I was looking forward to those. There was not a lot of travelling and we were playing in a format I knew I was good at. We beat Essex in our first game and then went down to Bristol and defeated Gloucestershire on a Sunday afternoon, June 5. I took 2 for 22 from four overs and bowled very well.

No dramas. Back to normal. Or so I thought.

Three days later I had another productive session with Brett Morrissey in London. Mark Robinson picked me up from Gatwick Airport Station and we drove to Chelmsford for the return game against Essex. The atmosphere there on T20 nights can be pretty unforgiving for the opposition. They get a lot of West Ham fans there and if you're fielding close to the boundary it's like being an opposition player at Upton Park. Not pleasant – and I'm a West Ham fan myself!

But if you get on top, it can go very quiet very quickly. We always seemed to thrive on the atmosphere there and that night was no different. We made 168 for 6 and then restricted them to 151 for 7. I bowled decently again and the team were playing well. We fancied ourselves in T20 that summer. Monty Panesar would open the bowling, we had some clever seamers and Lou Vincent had come in as a Kolpak player because he had a UK passport. He was a gun bat in the middle order and a very handy fielder.

I always struggled to get to sleep after a T20 game and I'm not alone. As a player, you'd either be on a big high after winning or, if you'd lost, you'd be dissecting the game bit by bit trying to work out what went wrong, especially if you were the captain. By the time we got back from Chelmsford and the adrenalin was starting to wear off it was nearly 3am before I nodded off. I had been feeling very tired for a couple of days. That was a warning but I chose to ignore it.

The following day we went up to London for one of Mark Davis's benefit functions at Lord's. I was sitting on a table surrounded by people I knew and had a lovely evening. A few glasses of wine, although nothing excessive, great food as always at headquarters and convivial company. But it was another late night.

A few days earlier I'd decided that I wanted to talk in depth about what had happened in the last few days before I'd come home from the World Cup and about my ongoing treatment, to unburden myself almost. Mark Robinson and the club were not that sure it was a good idea but I wanted to tell my story. I didn't want there to be any secrets, in the same way I had confronted the issue when I came home from the World Cup and the reasons why I had done so.

Sussex had received several requests for interviews in the preceding weeks but I wasn't keen on speaking to lots of different reporters or even doing a set-piece press conference. I wanted to talk to people I knew, who I could trust and who would tell my story sympathetically. I was going to speak to Bruce Talbot, a journalist I'd known throughout my Sussex career, who had followed the county for years for the local evening paper, the *Brighton Argus*, home and away. He had my permission to use parts of the interview if there was interest from the national press, which he explained there almost certainly would be. I also said I was willing to speak to Ian Ward, an old Sussex team-mate, on Sky Sports as my only broadcast interview. So at lunchtime on Friday, a few hours before we were due to play Middlesex at Hove in the T20, I spoke to Bruce for more than an hour. It all came out – the build-up to my breakdown in Sri Lanka, the history of my recent struggles with depression and what I was doing now to combat it. It felt good. Bruce was happy too. He'd got a very interesting story which he knew the national press would be interested in. He promised to make a donation to Mind, the mental health charity, from his fees.

The ground was packed for the Middlesex game with more than 5,000 in and it was a lovely evening. We scored 163 for 8 which we felt was a winning total on another slow pitch. I made 17 and when we went out to field I felt okay.

Then it started again.

I came on to bowl and Steven Crook started whacking me. My four overs cost 40 runs and I didn't bowl well at all in conditions which should have suited me. I started abusing him verbally, which he didn't deserve because he's a lovely bloke, and which was unusual behaviour for me. I was feeling more and more frustrated, with myself, with everything. To make matters worse I dropped a catch off Scott Newman, who went on to play a match-winning innings for Middlesex.

I didn't want to be there anymore. I remember standing at mid-wicket wishing the ground would open up and I could fall down a big black hole. There and then. In front of 5,000 people. The game was going on around me and I didn't have a clue what was happening. All I knew was that I wanted to be off the pitch as soon as possible. So that's what I did. I don't even think I asked the umpires' permission, which you are supposed to do. I ran off, up the stairs, into the dressing room and started crying my eyes out.

Karin was in the ground and a few moments later I felt her reassuring arms around me. The game was still going on but I was totally oblivious to it.

That was the first time I thought I might not be able to play cricket again. Ever. I wasn't around the England team anymore but if this was going to happen to me when I played for Sussex what did it mean for my future as a professional cricketer? How could I cope?

Karin smuggled me out of the ground and when asked about my unexpected departure by the press afterwards Mark Robinson told them I'd been taken ill. Which was true I guess. The interview with Ian Ward, planned for the next day, was cancelled and after thinking about it for a while I decided I didn't want my story appearing in the papers either. Robbo phoned Bruce Talbot, who was very good about it even though, he later told me, he'd written about 7,000 words that day when he was told at 11pm that the story would have to be canned.

Along with Karin, Kate Green had been at the Middlesex game and, realising something was wrong, had come up to the dressing room. I'd got to know Kate through her role as the personal development officer for both the ECB and the PCA, the players' union. I wasn't seeing Brett Morrissey every week anymore and it had becoming increasingly impractical for both of us – because he was based in Birmingham – to meet on a regular basis. She put me in touch with a psychotherapist who was based in Southampton, which was a lot easier to get to for me.

We met for a few months but by the end of 2011 I felt I was well enough not to see anyone. He was a massive cricket fan and when we met we'd spend the first half an hour or so just chatting about the game. I don't know whether this helped and while it was nice to have a chat about cricket I never really opened up about the other experiences in my life, which may have been causing me problems.

I didn't feel it was helping, all I wanted to talk about was Mike Yardy and my problems, my issues. To me, nothing else was important.

A couple of days after the Middlesex incident I reassured myself and the people around me that I was okay again. The truth was that I still hadn't entirely convinced myself that depression was not an illness that would just come and go, like a bout of flu.

I was putting on an act again. I had become concerned that if I didn't get back to playing quickly people would start to think I wouldn't be able to have any sort of career. I also thought the longer I left it I would end up convincing myself of that fact as well.

I played in a second-team game and would have nets at Hove early in the evening with Keith Greenfield, the club's academy director and a dear friend, when there was little chance of anyone else being around. I immersed myself in cricket again. Some players used to hate the nets but I never had a problem with practice. The harder I worked the better

I'd become and now I was trying to get back into a familiar routine. I was absolutely determined that I wanted to keep playing and yet, all the time, there was that voice in my head: "You do realise you might not be able to do this for much longer."

Five years on, I'm amazed at how I got through 2011 without another breakdown. My acting must have been Oscar-standard by the end of that season because there were lots of times when I felt as bad as I had that night at Hove.

Less than a month after the Middlesex game I made my first-team comeback in a T20 match against Glamorgan at Hove. No one apart from the close circle knew the real reason why I'd gone off during that match although I'm sure the press must have thought it strange that I didn't play again until 7 July 7. I bowled well, taking 1 for 25 from my four overs, but was dismissed for a duck. However, we won the game to move back into contention for a place in the quarter-finals.

Until now, the only emotion people had conveyed when I spoke about what I was going through was sympathy. But the following evening, when we played Kent at Canterbury, we were in the field when I heard this group of Kent supporters, who had clearly been enjoying a few beers, singing "Does your shrink know you're here?" over and over again. It didn't affect my performance. We were defending 159 in a game we had to win, restricted them to 144 for 8 and I took 1 for 29 and bowled well against a decent batting line-up. But it did surprise me and I sensed the embarrassment the Kent players felt as well. They all heard it.

Nothing was said that night but the following day, when we were training, Mark Robinson asked if I'd been aware of it. I said I had and that no harm had been done. I guess it was just ignorance, fuelled by a few beers. We all say stupid things when we've had a few, don't we? But Sussex were not happy and, to be fair, Kent were very good about it. They had received quite a few complaints from their own members and sent a letter of apology for what had happened. I was trying hard to keep things under the radar, but incidents like this, which thankfully were very rare, made me think I was undergoing something that was, in fact, very public. And prolonged public scrutiny was the last thing I wanted.

My last meeting with Brett took place at the end of July. We were playing Warwickshire and it was my first game which involved staying away from home. As usual, I had my own room as captain, and everything off the field went fine. On it we got our usual hammering at Edgbaston, a ground where Sussex hadn't won since 1981. To try and break the hoodoo we had even swapped to a different hotel from our normal one but it made little difference as we were beaten by an innings. But after scoring just two runs in the first innings I made an unbeaten half-century when we followed on, my first significant Championship score of the summer.

From our first meeting Brett had encouraged me to write down my feelings when I was having a difficult time. He used the analogy that if you tried to squash or suppress them they would always come back bigger. Someone told me that listening to mindfulness tapes would help so every time I went to the gym or for a walk I had that on my iPod. I understood what Brett was trying to do. He wanted to find a pattern of my thoughts.

I don't do either of those things now. Like everyone else, I have hundreds of thoughts during the day, some of them negative. My coping mechanism is simply to say to myself, 'see how you feel in an hour'. More often than not that helps. A lot of days I will be fine or the following day I will look back and think 'yesterday, you were really anxious and today you're okay'. They are fairly simple things but they work. I know now that the stressful situations and anxiety will stop. It won't go on for ever.

I was proud of how I finished that 2011 season. We were knocked out of the T20 in the quarter-finals by Lancashire at Hove, a huge disappointment although not entirely unexpected as we were severely understrength that night. Neither Murray Goodwin nor Luke Wright, our two best batsmen, played and we got nowhere near their 152 for 8. Similarly, Surrey, now coached by my former captain Chris Adams, did a number on us in the semi-final of the Clydesdale Bank 40-over competition at The Oval.

But I finished the Championship season strongly. I made a half-century in a losing cause against Worcestershire at Horsham but felt as fluent at the crease as I'd done for a long, long time in that game. A week later I had one of the matches I am proudest of when I scored a century in each innings against Yorkshire at Scarborough. Isn't the sea air meant to be a cure for ills and ailments? Possibly not in my case, but against a decent attack I made 130 and 122. I became the first visiting batsman to Yorkshire to score hundreds in both innings since Alan Jones, a former Sussex player, did it for Glamorgan at Middlesbrough in 1976. It was also the first instance of a Sussex player scoring two hundreds in the same game for ten years away from home. I enjoyed it immensely and so did my team-mates. They knew how much I had been through and was still going through and what it meant to me on a personal level. I may even have had a couple of beers to celebrate.

It was actually quite a bizarre game. A 75-year-old local gent had to umpire on the second day at square leg after Trevor Jesty went down with a stomach bug which affected a lot of us, myself included. Oh, and a young Yorkshire batsman called Joe Root made his first Championship hundred. The match itself looked to be heading for a draw but Yorkshire, who needed to win to keep their title hopes alive, decided to have a dart in the last hour at scoring 162 in 16 overs, having been set 344 to win in 55 after I'd declared our second innings on 333 for 6. Jacques Rudolph, their captain, asked who was going to bowl the next few overs. He was going to take his helmet off if I was going to bowl our part-time spinners. I did and he started to go on the attack. Obviously, if I'd known they were going to go for the runs I would have batted on. We needed the points to try and climb away from relegation trouble. They reached 312 for 6 with an over left before settling for a draw.

I finished the summer with 617 Championship runs at 44.07 from ten games which I was very proud of. As a side we had come up short, but since the Middlesex incident I had been okay. I knew the danger signs now and how to respond. It helped that as soon as the season was over I threw myself into a major rebuilding project which was taking place at the house. Then, in the early weeks of 2012, I flew to the West Indies to take part in a T20 tournament with Sussex. We had a young, fairly inexperienced side and got knocked out in the first round but I enjoyed the trip and there were no issues off the field. By then I had stopped seeing specialists. I felt okay and that my own coping strategies were keeping me on an even keel.

I even felt emboldened to write about my experiences of the previous 12 months. *Wisden Cricketers' Almanack* had approached me at the end of 2011 about writing something in the 2012 edition. Initially, I asked Bruce Talbot if he'd write it for me, based on an interview we would do, but a couple of days later I changed my mind. When I rang him he must have experienced a sense of déjà vu after what had happened in the previous summer. But no, I wasn't going to pull out. I still wanted to do it but I wanted to write it myself. Which I did. My words. Here's what I wrote:

> Cricket and Depression – An insider's tale
> The irony was that 2010 had been the most successful period of my career. I had helped England win the world Twenty20, established myself in the one-day side and, that summer, played in three series wins. But deep down I knew I was in a bad place. I was not enjoying what should have been a fantastic experience. I was very tense and living on an increasingly short fuse, both with myself and others.

I had always had high expectations, but things were getting out of hand. I could never please myself, was constantly striving for more and setting unrealistic goals, which just increased the pressure I was putting on myself. Because of the self-doubt, I would take things people said to me and twist them beyond all context. I would be looking for any comment to latch on to. "There you go Mike, told you so," I would think. "You're no good, you can't do it."

I was supposed to be living the dream. Instead, I felt angry with myself. Here, after all, was a scenario most people would love. I remember coming back to play for Sussex after a one-day international in July 2010 and having a couple of arguments with the umpire during a Twenty20 game against Essex. We played Hampshire and I was run out for nought. I walked past my batting partner and good friend Murray Goodwin and subjected him to a tirade of abuse, which I had never done before. I felt terrible afterwards.

A lot of things were happening which were out of character. I had always liked my own space, but now the very act of being around other people became an effort. My mind was saying, "They don't like you anyway. Why would they? You're a loser."

Everyone has negative thoughts but I was letting mine ruin my life. I joined up with the one-day squad to play Pakistan in September and, though it hurts to say so now, I wasn't really looking forward to it. I started the series well but my performances deteriorated, inevitable, perhaps, given my state of mind.

I had learned to put on a brave face but I woke up on the morning of the last one-dayer in Southampton and couldn't carry on. I didn't want to get out of bed. I just wanted to go home. I spoke to my wife, Karin, who knew I had been struggling. She was in a difficult position because she knew how hard I had worked to follow my dream but she was also aware, to a certain extent, of how I was feeling. I went to see Andy Flower, who was unbelievably supportive. It was a huge relief just to tell him. My place in that game went to my county colleague, Luke Wright.

Over the coming months I received great support from Brett Morrissey, a clinical psychologist recommended by Andy. I felt comfortable playing Twenty20 cricket for Central Districts in New Zealand before joining up with the one-day squad after the Ashes in 2011. I was anxious, but I knew I was better able to deal with things – even though my support network was on the other side of the world. I really started enjoying the experience of playing for England. I took the good days and bad days for what they were, and was really looking forward to the World Cup on the subcontinent. I had been there before and knew that, because of security, it would be difficult to get about. But I thought I could handle it.

After a few weeks, however, my mind started to win the battle and negative thoughts took over. Because I was not playing very well it had something to grip hold of.

Once more, I was fighting myself and rarely stopped to think I was taking part in a great tournament. At night, I would lie for hours battling with my mind. It became a vicious circle. I was missing my family, I was performing badly and my self-belief was low. The harder I tried the more I just kept hitting a brick wall. In many ways, all that time thinking was worse than the sleep deprivation.

When we arrived in Sri Lanka for our quarter-final I was struggling. I was out of the team and remember operating at a training session in a daze. Our spin-bowling coach Mushtaq Ahmed, a great friend and former Sussex team-mate, insisted that I needed to think of my health. At this point I knew I had to go home and spoke to Andy, who again was very understanding. I was desperate not to be a distraction before a big game, but I had been fighting this for so long. I just didn't have any fight left.

Why me? I'm not the most talented of players in any case. Now, on top of that, I was having to beat my mind first. I realise now that so many people face these challenges with no support. Millions suffer from depression and it's not simply a case of feeling in a bad mood. It can take over people's lives, it's not a weakness. I was gutted by the reaction of some individuals and could not believe people could be so judgemental. I accept critics could have a view on my cricket – but not this.

I have learned a lot about myself in the last year, and what I need to do to lead a happy life. I have had more bad times, but with every relapse I would learn more. I lost a huge amount of belief and at one stage doubted if I could play cricket to the level I wanted. I have been very lucky to have great support, both personally and professionally, but I believe deep down that you have to take on depression and its effects yourself; not fight, but outsmart it.

Now I feel much more content with myself and, by the end of the 2011 season, I was really starting to enjoy playing again. I know there will be days when I don't want to play cricket but this is something I have managed throughout my career. One thing is for sure, the bad days will never outweigh the great ones. I really do appreciate how lucky I am to be playing cricket for a living.

When the *Wisden* article appeared I did a few interviews and felt comfortable talking to the media, another sign that I was coping. The coverage was very sympathetic and when Sussex prepared for the 2012 season in Dubai I was feeling really positive. The previous 12 months had, at times, been stressful and traumatic but I was in a good place. There had been no further relapses and I felt we had an emerging team capable of challenging for trophies and, in the back of my mind, I hadn't entirely given up the thought of playing for England again, at least in the T20 format. But a few weeks into the season things took a turn for the worse. It was one of the hardest decisions of my life but for my own piece of mind, and to rediscover the pleasure of simply playing again, I had to give up the job I had coveted since the day I first became part of the Sussex cricket family. I couldn't be captain anymore.

4

Making it

I WAS the typical sporty kid growing up. Just ask Ruby. She was our elderly neighbour in the house in Winterbourne Close in Hastings where I grew up with Dad Howard, Mum Bev and my elder brother Rob, who was two years older than me.

There would be some sort of game in Winterbourne Close involving Rob and I and some of the local kids virtually every day, rain or shine. There wasn't a lot of traffic so passing cars didn't stop play too often and our house had a long drive which was perfect for summer days in our impromptu cricket net. The problem was that her house was on a slightly raised level so more often than not we would whack the ball into her front wall or front door. Or through as was once the case. Ruby, not surprisingly, was furious. Rob and I had to hide under the car.

I guess I was one of those kids whose generation were the last that spent the majority of their spare time outdoors. There were computer games around but we never spent too much time in front of the TV when we could be outside playing cricket or football. My first memories are of playing games in Winterbourne Close.

I came into the world on 27 November 1980. I was born in Pembury, on the Sussex–Kent border near Tunbridge Wells. Dad was a policeman and Mum worked providing care for the elderly. They divorced when I was 16 and it was quite messy, but until then they did all they could for me in terms of encouraging me to play sport and ferrying me here, there and everywhere to practice sessions.

It helped that Dad was a good standard club cricketer himself at Battle Cricket Club, a few miles from Hastings, although the first time I went there, for a kids' coaching course at the age six, there wouldn't have been any of the other children – or coaches for that matter – who thought there was a potential Sussex or England cricketer about to take their first steps in the game.

I was so bad that I ended up having my own private coaching – from a 16-year-old girl. Peter Finch was in charge of the sessions and Jackie, whose brother Jason is the father of current Sussex player Harry, used to go along to help out. Jackie had no pretensions as a cricketer herself, but she would lob the ball gently at me and I'd take a swing at it or she would throw some easy catches in my direction. Jackie eventually married Ian Gillespie, who taught me PE at secondary school, and for years every time I saw them, when I was breaking through at Sussex, they would take the mickey out of my embryonic efforts at picking up the basics of the game. But Jackie deserves a lot of credit in my story.

Dad was a right-handed opening batsman for Battle and I think he could have played at a higher standard, possibly Sussex League level. He set up Battle's first colts section when I was nine and it was then that my interest in cricket really took hold, well that and the long Saturday afternoons spent at the ground playing on the edge of the outfield with Rob or in the nets while Dad was in action. It was there that I fell in love with the game.

Dad's achievement in setting up a colts section is even more commendable when you consider that in a small town like Battle there wasn't a huge pool of young talent to call upon. Some of the better boys were already at nearby Hastings Cricket Club, whose youth section had been established for much longer, but it was certainly good for me to develop my game at Battle. From about the age of nine or ten I would be playing with boys much older than myself, even as old as 14 or 16 years, to make up the numbers. I remember facing Robin Martin-Jenkins, who was five years older than me, in a colts match against Horsham. I'd also be roped in on a Saturday to play adult cricket from the age of ten if someone dropped out of the team at short notice, which happened quite often.

That was good for me. I was quite big physically for my age and it certainly toughened me up. Even at that age I got quiet satisfaction if I hit an adult bowler for four, which happened more frequently than you might imagine because even at that age I had a bit of strength. It drove the opposition bowlers to distraction of course. Has a kid really just hit me back over my head for four?

There were some good young cricketers in Battle then, just not enough of them. And it didn't help that a couple of our friends, Tom Chaplin and Tim Rice-Oxley, were not always available on Saturday because they had band practice. They got some stick for that from the rest of us. Band practice? When they could have been playing cricket? What was all that about?

A few years later I found out. I was round at Robin Martin-Jenkins' flat in Hove having a drink when he stuck a CD on of a band I'd never heard of called Keane. "It's funny," he said, "because the singer is the brother of James Chaplin, your old captain at Hastings." The penny dropped. Tom and Tim had been putting Keane together when they should have been playing cricket for Battle. It was only when they kept having No.1 albums and singles that I finally forgave them!

As well as cricket I loved football. When I went to primary school at St Vincent's in Hastings I was in the school XI at the age of nine, playing either in central midfield or up front. I played for the district team and was put forward for a trial at Brighton & Hove Albion's Centre of Excellence, but it came to nothing.

We used to play against another local school called St Paul's and it was then that I came up against this tall central midfielder who I would encounter again when we ended up together at William Parker Secondary School. His name was Gareth Barry and he has gone on to have a stellar career, playing for Aston Villa, Manchester City and Everton and winning 53 England caps. Gareth was only four months younger than me and although we weren't best friends we forged quite a healthy mutual respect when it became evident at William Parker that he was developing into a good footballer and I was making my way with the same speed in cricket.

I guess it is quite surprising that a school in Hastings, which let's face it is a bit of backwater, had produced two international sportsmen but William Parker had a great reputation for sport. Before I arrived Kevin Ball, who played in the Premier League for Sunderland and Fulham, and the former Sussex spinner Nicky Phillips had been educated there and, after Gareth and I left, it produced two more top-flight footballers in Dean Hammond and Steve Cook, who is at Bournemouth in the Premier League these days.

I played a bit of County League football for a local team, Westfield, but by the age of 15 or 16 I was only doing it for enjoyment. I played a couple of first-team matches but when I was dropped for not turning up for a training session because I had cricket practice I couldn't understand why. As far as football was concerned, I could take it or leave it.

The same could quite possibly be said about my academic studies. I wasn't thick by any means but I was lazy. I scraped five GCSEs and two A Levels, one of which was in sports science, something which came in handy when my professional cricket career finished nearly two decades later. There was a practical element to the course which appealed and in the summer of 1996 I would go around schools all over East Sussex with my best mate Greg Hobbs providing basic cricket coaching for the kids. Now Greg wasn't the best cricketer so I'd play and miss all the time to make him look good and when the youngsters came on to bowl I'd hit them all over the playing field.

At career guidance evenings I was more often than not pointed towards the armed forces. Hmm, Private Yardy. Not sure about that. Anyway, when I was 16 and was just to go on my first tour with the Sussex Young Cricketers there was only one career I was interested in. I had been playing for Sussex since under-11s as a left-arm opening bowler who batted somewhere in the middle order. At that age the sheer physical act of propelling the ball 22 yards down a normal-sized pitch at even gentle pace is quite difficult, so when I played for Battle's adult teams I had to learn fast.

I'd gone to Hove for my first Sussex trial at the age of ten, nurtured by Pat Cale, who looked after a generation of young cricketers at the club. Pat was a lovely man but initially I didn't feel that I fitted in. Most of my contemporaries were privately educated and they knew each other from playing in public school matches. I'm not sure what they made of a little scrapper from Hastings turning up. I remember one early game for Sussex under-11s against Kent when a lad came all the way from Chichester and bowled just a solitary over while the coach's son batted through the innings and then took the new ball. It was totally unfair, but you could hardly make a protest and be seen to be rocking the boat.

The following year, 1991, we had a lovely guy called Stan Berry coaching us and it was a lot more enjoyable. I picked up the end of season batting award and although we only won a couple of games Stan made it a lot of fun and ensured everyone had an opportunity. To be fair, it wasn't a vintage crop of young players. Of my team-mates, Mark Nash – Sussex opener Chris's elder brother – and Luke Marshall played second-team cricket and Krishnah Singh had some games for Loughborough University a few years later but I remember the coaches being every excited about a young lad from Brighton College called Matt Prior, who had come to Sussex when his parents moved from South Africa. By the time I was in the under-14s Matt, who was a couple of years younger than me, and Carl Hopkinson were already both in our team.

Sussex had decided to replace the old indoor school at the southern end of the ground with a new purpose-built facility. For one winter that meant junior nets and practice were moved to Arundel. My parents had split up and getting a lift there wasn't always practical, although it never crossed my mind that I didn't need to make the effort to get there from Hastings, even though it involved a three-hour journey via Gatwick Airport which ended with me lugging my kit, rain or shine, up the hill for a mile or so to the Castle Ground from Arundel Station. I did it for the odd midweek squad session too, although Mum would often come and pick me up and ensure I didn't get back home at the same time as the milk was being delivered. Nevertheless, even by car, it was quite a hike.

I was 15 when I first thought I had a good chance of being a professional. Keith Greenfield, who had just taken over as second team captain, and Chris Waller gave me some positive feedback. I knew I was the best player in my age group and I could see I was better than quite a few older lads as well. By then I had left Battle to join Hastings Priory, who played in the Sussex League on one of the best wickets in the county. All my contemporaries in the Sussex under-15s had moved to bigger clubs and it felt like a natural progression. I had begun to dominate bowling attacks in the East Sussex League and had averaged 70 in my last season there. It was time to test myself in a better standard.

I was 15 when I made my second-team debut for Sussex. They had arranged two one-day friendlies against the MCC Young Professionals at Hastings at the end of the 1996 season. James Chaplin, my captain at Hastings, played but the team was comprised mainly of Sussex professionals. To be honest, I don't remember the standard being a massive step up from league cricket. In the first game I took 2 for 29, including the wicket of Nick Wilton, who was later on the professional staff with me at Sussex, and scored 33. The following day I got the MCC captain and coach Clive Radley out, which was a decent scalp, and picked up another couple of wickets. I remember the thrill of scoring my first boundary and taking those wickets. It did feel that I was on my way.

That winter I went on my first overseas cricket tour to Barbados with Sussex Young Cricketers. It was a great experience because however hard the coaches tried to instil a sense of discipline into us it still felt like a fantastic holiday, playing cricket in the sunshine with a lot of mates who you'd grown up with in the Sussex junior set-up. Things got a little out of hand one night when we found ourselves in a bar next to a restaurant where the coaches, Keith Greenfield and Chris Waller, were enjoying a quiet meal. One of the lads, James Chadburn, had a bit too much rum punch and ended up being sick on the beach.

Keith was furious, not so much because he had thrown up but that the rest of us had seen this happen and basically left James to it. We were punished for not looking out for one of our team-mates with a 5am fitness session the next day. Lesson learned.

I wanted to get out of William Parker as soon as I could but, deep down, I realised at the age of 17 that I wasn't ready yet to be a professional cricketer. I still hadn't nailed down my role in the second team, where I appeared sporadically during 1997 in between finishing off my exams. I was first and foremost a top four batsman, who could bowl a bit of seam-up as well but often I would find myself shunted down the order, sometimes as low as eight or nine, to make way for first-team players seeking a bit of form against modest second XI bowling attacks. At that stage I wasn't sure I was good enough to make the step up and the county were hardly encouraging the development of their own players by looking at players released by other counties to rebuild the professional squad after six capped players, including captain Alan Wells, had left in the winter of 1996/97 and a new committee had been installed under the chairmanship of Robin Marlar.

It had been a while since a decent batsman had come through the club's junior ranks. James Kirtley and Jason Lewry, recruited from Goring after his phenomenal exploits in club cricket, had emerged as promising bowlers but the batting stocks were pretty thin, hence Sussex's decision to eventually recruit the likes of Chris Adams from Derbyshire, Northamptonshire's Richard Montgomerie and Tony Cottey from Glamorgan, all experienced, reliable batsmen in need of a new challenge and, in Grizzly's case, a captain who went on to lead Sussex to a remarkable period of success, which I was lucky to be part of.

But the coaches, including I guess Peter Moores who was now in charge, must have seen some raw potential in MH Yardy and at the start of 1999 I was offered my first professional deal on what was then called a retainer contract. I would get a squad number and be made to feel part of the professional set-up but the pay was pretty poor. I signed my first contract for £3,000 although there was an incentive of £100 for every day I played in the first team. I must have been confident that first-team opportunities would arise quickly because I signed it without hesitation. No agents involved, no family there. I just signed on the dotted line. I might not have felt worthy of the title yet, but I could now call myself a professional cricketer.

Now came the hard part – proving that I was good enough to be in the professional ranks. I was still living in Hastings and hadn't passed my driving test but James Kirtley, who lived in Eastbourne, took me under his wing a bit. He'd pick me up from Eastbourne Station every day when we were training and in those first few months, as we drove to Hove, we talked cricket incessantly and he became something of a mentor to me. He was five years older and had established himself in the first team and I admired the way he prepared so assiduously for a day's cricket or even a training session. He was always so focussed on what he wanted to achieve, both from the day in front of us and his career as a whole. I so much wanted to be like that. James was quite quiet and kept himself to himself, a bit like me, but he gave me so much good advice.

I remember a one-day game at Hove in 2001 when James was captain because Chris Adams was injured. We'd invariably talk tactics during the car journeys to and from Hove so when he turned to me at mid-off during the match and asked whether we should have fine leg up and deep square back it felt quite good that my opinions were being sought by the skipper. Then a few seconds later, as he walked back to his mark just as I was about to offer my pearls of wisdom, he turned to me again. "On second thoughts Yards, what the fuck do you know?" I made 50 that day which made me feel better!

I wasn't even established in the second team during my first year on the staff in 1999. I only played in five Second XI Championship games and didn't score a half-century so I was surprised when I was told I was going to make my first-team debut on 14 August in a day-night game against Sri Lanka A. The county had just installed permanent floodlights at Hove which weren't great to play under and in an attempt to try and attract a crowd they decided to use orange balls and green stumps. There were only about 200 people there to see me bowl six wicketless overs for 31 and get run out for two as we lost a rain-interrupted match by nine runs on Duckworth/Lewis. Still, I'd climbed another rung on the ladder.

A rite of passage for all young cricketers is to go overseas and play. In the winter of 1999/2000 a lad I knew in Hastings called Richard Burnett fixed it up for me to go to Cape Town to turn out for Western Province. There was only one place in their first XI for an overseas player but you could have as many as you wanted in the seconds. Two other English pros went as well – Andy Patterson, a young Irish wicketkeeper-batsman who had a brief career with Sussex – and Glenn Roberts, the Derbyshire batsman. I was looking forward to playing and training in the sunshine but, almost as soon as I'd arrived, the competition rules were changed and it was decided only one overseas player would be allowed in the second XI as well.

The prospect of playing in the third or fourth teams didn't appeal, because I knew the standard would be no better than Battle. A couple of weeks after arriving I decided to try and find a new club. Vincent Barnes, who went on to assist Mickey Arthur when he was in charge of the South Africa team, was one of the Western Province coaches and he suggested I get in contact with Victoria CC, an all black team based in one of the townships, where I did some training.

The Victoria players were brilliant towards me but I left there and ended up playing for Cape Town CC, initially in their fourths before earning a promotion to the second team. The games were two-day matches played on successive Saturdays and I remember arriving for my debut, against an all black team, to find a stolen car burning on the edge of the outfield. The Cape Town lads just got on with it, changing out of their cars before enjoying the game. I must admit, the thought of going back the following weekend to finish the match had me fretting for days beforehand.

Richard, who had felt bad about leaving me high and dry at Western Province, arranged for me to stay with a guy called Russell Adams, who had played at Hastings. In return for my bed and board in his garage annex I painted his roof. I linked up with the Sussex Academy early in 2000 when they came over on tour and I did a few days at Newlands bowling in the nets to the likes of Jacques Kallis and Herschelle Gibbs, who were playing in the Test series against England, and Hylton Ackerman. Those few months were certainly an interesting life experience but I can't say my cricket improved as much as I'd hoped.

The new millennium dawned with me wondering if I could make the next step up at Sussex. My contract was due to expire at the end of 2000 and although I got a bit more of a taste of the first-team environment that summer I certainly didn't feel part of the set-up. It was a bad year for Sussex. We finished bottom in the County Championship, having been in the Division Two promotion positions until August, after things really started to unravel when we played Glamorgan at Colwyn Bay towards the end of that month.

I'll always remember it of course because it was there that I made my Championship debut. I only played in six Second XI Championship games that summer but a few days before I scored 94 in a game against Kent at Hastings before getting out to James Tredwell, a future England team-mate of course. A couple of days later I was included in the squad for a one-day match against Northamptonshire at Eastbourne but wasn't selected. Afterwards, though, five players, Wasim Khan, Toby Peirce, Shaun Humphries, Andy Patterson and Justin Bates, were all told they wouldn't be offered new contracts at the end of the season. With promotion hopes disappearing Peter Moores and Chris Adams decided to invest in youth and give me a chance. On Monday morning I was told I would be playing after nets. I went back to the dressing room to get my gear and found a note on my kit from Wasim, wishing me all the best. A nice touch and something I would always remember.

I drove up to North Wales that afternoon to meet up with the rest of the squad for a team meeting. Well, that was the plan anyway. Unfortunately, Umer Rashid and Billy Taylor, who were travelling together, weren't great navigators. They arrived about four hours after the rest of us having taken a detour through Worcester and Cardiff. "We thought it was near Swansea," Umer explained when he finally got to Llandudno at the other end of Wales later that night.

It wasn't a great game to make my Championship debut. Grizzly won the toss and got seduced by a brownish-coloured pitch and stuck them in. Steve James and Matthew Elliott, the Australian opener, easily saw off James Kirtley and Jason Lewry's new-ball spells but when Mark Robinson came on as first change the consensus among the senior pros in the slip cordon – I was fielding at third slip – was that the pitch would be ideal for a wicket-to-wicket bowler like Robbo who got a bit of nip off the surface. It was either first or second ball that Elliott launched him onto the bank at the far end of the ground for six and not much longer after that we dispensed with a third slip, then a second and, by the end of the day, any slip at all.

Glamorgan made 718 for 3 declared with Steve James scoring a triple hundred. I recall going out to open the batting with Richard Montgomerie shortly before tea on the second day, looking at the tiny scoreboard in the corner of the ground, and thinking the scorers had made a mistake. The most runs I'd ever seen scored in second-team cricket was around 400. Peter had done me a favour before the game and told me I would be playing in the last three games of the season so I didn't feel under too much pressure. I felt confident I could make the step up but I was blown away. Alex Wharf, who I ended up going on an England A tour with, got me out in both innings as we lost heavily and then when we played Nottinghamshire at Trent Bridge I had to face Paul Reiffel, who was a high-class operator back then. He got me for a duck in the first dig but I at least managed a nought not out in the second innings of a game which was rain-affected. I felt a bit overawed. Here was this good Australian fast bowler who I'd seen on the TV many times get far better players than me out. How was I meant to survive against this class of bowler, never mind score off him?

I fared a little better in our final home game of the season, scoring 14 and 12, but we lost inside two days to Gloucestershire and finished bottom of Division Two. The club had arranged for the end of season awards to be presented from the committee-room balcony afterwards which, as you can imagine, was a pretty sombre occasion. Surprisingly, quite a few people hung around and a few of the more vocal Sussex supporters were calling for Grizzly and Peter, or both, to be sacked. Fortunately, the chairman Don Trangmar held his nerve although I know there were people on the committee at the club who wanted there to be a change.

My own future was only slightly more certain. I had been offered a new contract and Peter told me I would be paid £8,500 a year, which was a big increase on my retainer of three grand. But when the contract was sent to me to sign the amount had been changed to £6,000. All through my life, if I feel I have been the subject of an injustice I have confronted it so I arranged to see Peter and Dave Gilbert, the chief executive. Dave tore into me, reducing me to tears. The gist of his argument was I was lucky to have a contract at all after the season we'd had. To be fair to Peter, he wasn't in a great position to back me up. There was no love lost between him and Dave and after the season Sussex had endured he was under pressure for his own job. So I signed the £6,000 contract without further complaint but, once the dust had settled and he knew he had a future at the club, Peter managed to find another £1,000 in travelling expenses for me because I was still in Hastings, living with my brother Rob, and still hadn't passed my driving test.

Dave and Peter also laid into me about my physical condition. I'd never been thin and I loved my grub and fortunately for me Sussex had just employed a lovely guy called Rob Harley, a sports scientist who worked at the University of Sussex's campus in Eastbourne. Rob had started to design tailor-made fitness and conditioning programmes for the players and I did a lot of sessions with him. I also embarked on my own end-of-season boot camp. My mum had just moved to the north of Scotland, about an hour from Inverness, after getting remarried so I moved in with her and her new husband for a month and trained every day, running up and down the picturesque highland hills and glens. I lost more than a stone during the winter and when I came back for pre-season training at the start of 2001 I looked like a different person.

Just as importantly I felt like a new person. If I had come back having made a few technical adjustments to my game I don't think Peter, Grizzly or the other lads would have noticed. But when the new slimmed-down Mike Yardy appeared everyone was amazed. I wasn't the tubby left-hander who'd looked out of his depth at the end of the 2000 season anymore. Although sport in general was making huge strides at the time in terms of looking after their athletes the only gauge of fitness that generation of players still knew was the dreaded bleep test. True, it was better than the rudimentary pre-season fitness regimes that Les Lenham, who had played for Sussex in the 1950s and 1960s before becoming the county batting coach, told us about. They seemed to involve nothing more than putting as many layers on as possible and completing laps of the outfield. But when I started to feature well in the bleep test results I was thrilled. Pete, who hadn't seen me much during the winter because he'd been coaching an England A tour in the West Indies, was impressed. Pete was as fit as most of the players and knew the sacrifices I'd made. I felt confident I would be in the team at the start of the season.

We went to the Caribbean for a pre-season camp in Grenada. There were four players, Dominic Clapp, Jamie Carpenter, Bas Zuiderent and Will House, who we'd signed from Kent in the winter of 1999/2000, whom I regarded as a rival for one, possibly two batting spots. I made some runs in the friendlies we played but when we got back to Hove and took part in another warm-up match Clapp, House and Zuiderent were all chosen even though a few senior players were injured and our overseas player, Murray Goodwin, hadn't arrived. I felt a bit demoralised but tried to react positively. I told Keith Greenfield, who was second XI coach, that if I was chosen in the seconds I wanted to open the batting to get the best possible exposure. I could easily have hidden down in the middle order and faced the change bowlers and fattened my average that way. It worked, but only after poor old Keith had copped a load of abuse from a few of us during an early-season second XI match against Warwickshire at Shirley, a club ground on the outskirts of Birmingham.

On the night we arrived Keith decided a team meal would be a good way of bonding the disaffected 'senior' players with the youngsters in the team. Bad move. Bas Zuiderent, who had only averaged just over 20 in the seconds in 2000, had been chosen for the opening Championship game against Worcestershire at New Road, the same match in which Matt Prior made his Sussex debut. Up the road at Shirley, Clapp, Carpenter and House were giving Keith both barrels about that selection, the gist being 'how has he been chosen instead of us?' To be fair, Bas was a great player to watch. He was a very stylish batsman but never scored runs on a consistent basis. I didn't harangue Keith at all, figuring that if I got a score against Warwickshire seconds I'd give myself a better chance. I made 49 on a difficult early-season club wicket and I think I impressed Keith that I'd toughed it out and not given it away. A couple of weeks later I was in the first team again for the Benson & Hedges Cup game against Middlesex at Hove and scored 59 from 67 balls. I was away.

People who followed my career always think that 2005 was the year I really blossomed. It's easy to believe that. After all, I fundamentally changed my technical approach to both batting and bowling and reaped the rewards with more than 1,500 first-class runs and England A selection at the end of the season. But I always regard 2001 as my breakthrough year. I played in 15 Championship games and although my best score was 87 not out against Hampshire at Arundel I averaged 34.80 and scored 990 first-class runs. At the start of the season Peter Moores had told me that the benchmark average for a young player was 30 and I had exceeded that.

The team were successful too. I'd grown up thinking Sussex were crap because they never seemed to win anything, but here I was part of a good team, with a nice mix of senior players and youngsters, sweeping all before them in Division Two of the County Championship. We won the title by beating Gloucestershire at Hove in the final game and the scenes afterwards could not have been more marked from 12 months previously. Murray Goodwin was an outstanding success and he, Richard Montgomerie and Chris Adams all scored heavily. Our 'awesome foursome' of seam bowlers – James Kirtley, Jason Lewry, Mark Robinson and Robin Martin-Jenkins – proved to be the best attack in the division by some distance. They all offered something different and if all else failed I could be relied on to come on and bowl some skiddy left-arm seam-up. I took eight wickets that season in all competitions and while I didn't have any sort of reputation as a golden arm I did okay.

And that was the thing. I didn't want to just be okay. I wanted to improve even more. Every team needed batsmen who could guts it out in tough conditions and I certainly fitted that stereotype at the time but I always knew I was capable of being a much more expansive cricketer, both with bat and ball. Peter Moores used to say that players whom he felt were putting too much pressure on themselves to perform needed to 'free themselves up' and I guess I was one of those.

At least I had the security of a contract to make those changes. The hierarchy at Hove must have been impressed with my progress because halfway through the 2001 season Dave Gilbert called me into his office and offered me a new deal through to the end of 2003 on £15,000 a year. I'd nearly trebled my wages and thought I'd won the lottery. Mind you I was still living in Hastings, hadn't yet passed my driving test and was being ferried in every day from Eastbourne by James Kirtley. At least now I could afford to give him a bit of petrol money.

5

No pain, no gain

IT had taken them 164 years, but Sussex finally won the County Championship for the first time in 2003. We had a great team led by a captain, Chris Adams, who built a side largely in his own image. We worked harder than the other teams, we trained harder and we prepared better. And we had the X factor, a little leg-spinner called Mushtaq Ahmed who did more for me and my game than any other team-mate during my career.

We'd got a glimpse of what he could offer towards the end of the 2002 season when Mushy played a couple of games as a short-term replacement for his Pakistan compatriot Saqlain Mushtaq for Surrey, including one at Hove. I wasn't involved in the match but the other lads were impressed, particularly Grizzly who'd faced him on the last day with Murray Goodwin and got through a crucial session unscathed to set up the victory – one of only three we achieved that season – that effectively made sure we would stay in Division One in our first season after promotion. Mushy wasn't fully fit but he could still bowl and as soon as he came off the pitch at the end of the game Grizzly and Peter Moores knew they had to sign him. Convincing the committee was harder but the chairman, Don Trangmar, always backed Grizz and Pete when he could. He had been under pressure to sack one or both of them when we finished bottom of everything in 2000 but had stuck with them and now he supported their judgement and told them to sign Mushy.

Having been bombed out of Somerset, and with his Pakistan career as good as finished, I guess Mushy was just grateful for a second chance in county cricket. He didn't realise it at the time and neither did I but I learned so much from facing him in the nets over the next five years or so. Picking his googly and actually playing him with a degree of competence was a minor triumph in itself for all of us batsmen at Sussex. And if he got me out I knew I wasn't alone and that it didn't count. By the end of 2003 he'd taken 103 Championship wickets. He made a lot of batsmen far better than I was back then look like complete novices.

But what he did teach me, and which I used when I switched from bowling seam to spin a couple of years later, was to try and develop a spin bowler's attacking mentality. Even in one-day cricket he was always on the hunt for wickets. Saqlain, who also had a season with us after leaving Surrey mainly in our one-day team because of his dodgy knees, was the same. If either of them got hit for a couple of boundaries their response was to bring in another close catcher, inviting the batsman to take another risk. Mushy got lots of wickets that way he could sense fear and loved to second guess his opponent. When I played for England Graeme Swann was exactly the same. More often than not my role would be different to Swann. I was more of a containing bowler but watching Mushtaq at work during his years with Sussex got me thinking about the way some spinners were always attacking, and how I could be a handy foil at the other end.

Mushy was the most selfless cricketer I ever played with. He wanted to help everyone and was the ultimate team man and he always looked out for me, especially in his first couple of years at Sussex when I was still finding my way in the game. We'd work on batting and bowling and he never tried to over-complicate things. It was great to link up with him again when I got in the England team and it's no surprise that he's developed into a world-class coach. I thought it was a loss to England when he left our set-up to join Pakistan's, although it was entirely understandable that he wanted to spend more time at home with his family. Being on the international treadmill for any length of time is a gruelling experience for players, but remember they can occasionally miss matches or even an entire series. That's not normally an option for a coach if he wants to keep his job, never mind prolong his career.

Playing for England was nothing but an idle dream for me at the start of 2002. Having broken through in 2001 I started the year well with 93 against Surrey and 73 against Somerset at Hove. But then I endured a run of low scores when I didn't seem to be able to get past 30. We arrived at Taunton in mid-July for the return Championship fixture and the wicket was an absolute road. I'd got to 36 just before the close on the second day and driving at Keith Dutch, the off-spinner, in the final over of the day I felt the ligaments at the back of my knee go. I hobbled out again the next day dosed up with painkillers but was out straight away. At least someone cashed in on the conditions though. Robin Martin-Jenkins made 205 and Mark Davis 111 and we ended up winning by an innings, one of those precious three victories that kept us up that season.

We did well to regroup and survive considering the awful start to the year we had all endured. Returning to Grenada for pre-season for the second time, our talented all-rounder Umer Rashid and his brother Burhan drowned whilst swimming in a deep pool at a place called Concord Falls on the other side of the island on Easter Monday. It had been a rare day off and the rest of the squad and coaching staff had spent the afternoon relaxing by the side of the hotel pool. Richard Montgomerie took the call at the pool bar and the rest of that day became a bit of a blur. I remember Peter Moores getting the squad together a couple of hours later, once the news had been confirmed by the local authorities, to tell us what had happened. A few minutes after that he had to ring their parents before they had found out through the media back in England. It was an extraordinarily brave thing for Peter to do, although entirely typical of him.

A year earlier I'd visited the falls with Monty and James Kirtley and dived in where the brothers had drowned – and I couldn't even swim. It was hard to imagine that they had both perished in an area the size of an average lounge. Their deaths shocked me as much as anyone but my coping mechanism was different. I preferred to be on my own and was more concerned with the effect it had on other members of the squad, particularly the lads like Bas Zuiderent and Billy Taylor to whom Umer was particularly close.

Umer died a few days after Ben Hollioake, the Surrey and England all-rounder, had lost his life in a car accident in Perth, Western Australia. Umer had a talent to rival Ben's, I have no doubt about that. I think he would have been the ideal cricketer for the T20 age because he did things differently and could improvise with both bat and ball. Sussex have suffered more than their share of tragedy over the years. All those who played with or knew him were devastated when Matt Hobden, our promising young fast bowler, was killed in tragic circumstances at the start of 2016. I'm sure Matt's memory will be cherished as warmly as Umer's has been by everyone at the club. They were both talented cricketers but will also be remembered by all of us as being special people. They never bore grudges and they always had an optimistic view of life which would rub off on others.

I finished 2002 with 794 first-class runs at an average of 28.35, a poorer return than in 2001. Second-season syndrome? Probably. What I was acutely aware of was that I hadn't made the same progress as guys like Matt Prior and

Tim Ambrose. Matt's stats weren't a great deal better than mine to be honest but he was capable of playing some eye-catching knocks and there was a bit of a buzz around him. With the benefit of hindsight, I was being unfair on myself by comparing myself with two guys who were obviously more talented but I knew a lot of players who had gone backwards after what they thought was their breakthrough season and I had been desperate to avoid it and to kick on instead.

In one-day cricket I made some decent contributions with both bat and ball but by the end of it I hadn't really progressed my one-day cricket at all. I took 3 for 30, my best limited-overs figures at the time, in a Benson & Hedges Cup quarter-final against Warwickshire at Hove but it turned out to be one of the most disappointing days I had in a Sussex shirt. They were a strong side and on a pretty average wicket we ended up with 196 for 7 from our 50 overs, which included 22 off 19 balls from me at No.8. We had Warwickshire struggling on 96 for 5 but then it rained for more than an hour which left us with a dilemma – go back out and try and win the game that day or come back in the morning. Peter Moores strongly felt we should go for the first option and it seemed the right thing to do at the time because all the momentum was with us. Another quick wicket or two and we'd have won. The problem was we ended up bowling with a wet ball and Ian Bell produced a superb knock of 85 not out to see them to victory with eight balls to spare the following morning. Nearly, but not quite. It summed up my season and to a certain extent Sussex's.

We knew more or less as soon as he turned up to join us at the start of 2003 that Mushy was going to make a massive difference to us. I remember watching him get a load of wickets in a pre-season game against Cardiff UCCE. The students didn't have a clue against him but in the nets a lot of our best players were struggling as well. We would get better against him, because we all came to enjoy facing him during practice, but virtually from the first game of the season unsuspecting county batsmen were caught like rabbits in the headlights.

I played two Championship games during that historical season. Of course I'd have loved to have been involved more in what was a fantastic summer for Sussex, our first Championship title in 164 years, but long-term not being in the team probably saved my career. It was the year I realised that if I couldn't make the improvements I needed to my game I'd rather pack up cricket and go and do something else instead. I didn't just want a career as a jobbing county player – I wanted to achieve things, win trophies and, yes, to play for England. If I couldn't make myself good enough to do that, with the help of the coaching staff at Sussex and through my own inner belief, then I wouldn't do it at all.

It's odd that one of my two games that season, which ended in a defeat, is still talked about by Sussex supporters as one of the turning points of that triumphant summer. I got into the team because Tony Cottey was injured for our game against Surrey at The Oval in May. They were a strong side and were favourites for the title. Even then, with relatively

little experience heind me, I relished the challenge. The
pitch was a belter and hard work for bowlers. Even Mushy
struggled. He did get Graham Thorpe out but only after he'd
made 156 out of a Surrey total of 480. I batted at three and
was caught in the slips by Thorpe off Jimmy Ormond for a
six-ball duck in the first innings. We ended up with 307 but
Ian Ward made a century in the second innings, leaving us to
chase 407 in a day and a bit.

When I was last out for 69, having batted through virtually
all of the final day, we were only five overs from a heroic
draw. 69 in five hours. 'Typical Yards' most people would
have thought at the time and they were right. I was proud of
the way I battled against a quality bowling attack but I also
knew I was capable of a lot more than that sort of stodgy
innings. And in any case, two days later Cotts was back in
the team when we beat Kent at Tunbridge Wells and my
only other Championship appearance that summer came in
a rain-affected drawn game at Trent Bridge in late July. I made
47 in our only innings but actually bowled quite well. I sent
down 13 overs in their second dig for 50 runs but didn't take
a wicket.

As a part-time bowler I was aware that I needed, if nothing
else, to have something of a reputation of a partnership breaker,
but tidy though those figures against Nottinghamshire
were the 'W' column was still blank. I remember Richard
Montgomerie, who bowled his off-spinners on very rare
occasions, got Kevin Pietersen out towards the end of that
game and feeling just a tinge of jealousy! In 12 List A matches

that summer I only picked up a single wicket. As a bowler, I was going nowhere either. I'd rather have been a crap bowler who got batsmen out caught on the boundary. At least I would have had another facet to my game that might have increased my chances of playing. I knew I was being judged on statistics and mine were not great.

Our strongest XI certainly did not include me and as the season reached its climax, with Sussex needing to beat Leicestershire at Hove in our final game to win the Championship, I didn't really feel part of all the celebrations at all. Any professional sportsman in a similar situation who says they would is not being honest with themselves. Peter Moores and Chris Adams did their best to make everyone on the fringes feel they had played their part and I suppose I had made a bit more of a contribution than some. I was 12th man for the title-winning game and spent most of the third day on the field covering for the lads who had enjoyed the long night of celebrations the previous evening in the Sussex Cricketer pub next to the ground. I know a lot of the lads can remember in minute detail what they did, where they went and how much they drank the day Sussex ended their 164-year wait to win the trophy that mattered.

My abiding memory is standing in the pub garden and seeing Mushy, the player who'd done more than anyone to get us over the line, driving slowly out of the ground in his sponsored people-carrier with his wife and family as if it was the end of a normal day's play. His Muslim faith forbade him from drinking alcohol but I'm sure he had a couple of cans of Coke, his tipple of choice, to toast his achievement. That, and a very long sleep. He'd certainly earned his rest at the end of that season.

Once the celebrations, the dinners and open-top bus parades were over I sat down with Pete and Mark Robinson for my end of season appraisal. I told them I wanted to make some fundamental changes to the way I batted. I had done a bit of tinkering in the nets and found that by taking guard outside leg stump and making a more exaggerated trigger movement back into the line of the ball I could hit straighter and harder. I didn't suddenly have a hugely bigger range of shots – that would come when I did some more work in the summer of 2004 – but I felt instantly freed-up and more confident. There were a few setbacks to endure first but having decided to fundamentally change the way I batted I finally had some clarity and a sense of purpose. I felt I could make myself a better batsman and fulfil the potential I knew I had, even though I accepted it wasn't going to happen quickly.

I practised hard that winter of 2003/04 but more importantly I practised smarter. I decided that even if I made some major alterations to my game I didn't want to spend day after day in the nets. When I did work with the other lads they noticed straight away that I was hitting the ball harder, never mind that I was facing the bowler with this slightly cock-eyed stance.

But all the time I was practising I wasn't earning any money and I was absolutely potless. In January 2003, I'd met Karin when I was at Aston University in Birmingham visiting a pal. She was studying French and when she left that summer we decided to rent a flat together in Redhill, so it would be easier for her to commute to London where she was hoping to start her career. She then got a good job with EDF Energy – based in Hove! But we had taken a lease on the Redhill flat and lived there through that winter while I worked part-time in a sports shop at Gatwick Airport to bring a few extra quid in.

With rent and bills to pay I needed that job. It was only when I got paid a bonus for winning the Championship that I managed to sort my finances out but working there also meant I didn't spend all my time thinking about cricket and the changes I was making to my game. I had been guilty in the early years of over-analysing things – my technique, how I adapted to certain situations in matches – far too much. Being in the nets all the time the previous winter had merely exacerbated the problem. Now, practice and net sessions were precious time and as that winter progressed and the 2004 season came closer I felt I had got the balance right. I knew what I wanted to achieve and how I could do it.

First of all, though, I had to get into the team. We had signed Ian Ward, the opening batsman from Surrey, for the title defence so I knew I wouldn't start the season but I did think that when I began playing competitive games with my new stance that it wouldn't be long before I got my rewards. How wrong I was. We played Nottinghamshire in a friendly at Hove and after getting a duck I saw my bowling, which I'd also done some work on during the winter, get absolutely smashed by Kevin Pietersen. He hit one ball through the covers so hard that James Kirtley, who was fielding there, took his hand out of the way to save himself from a broken finger. That's a criminal offence even on the village green but I couldn't blame him. Then, to round off a day to remember, I had to go back to Redhill in the evening and clear out the flat with Karin. Happy days!

We played MCC in the annual curtain-raiser at Lord's against the champion county. I was due to be 12th man but Chris Adams dropped out through illness and I got a last-minute call-up. I came in at No.8 in our first innings and after hitting Graham Napier to the boundary he had me caught behind next ball. I felt very low. But then something clicked. The pitch flattened out and we went in again 339 runs in arrears and saved the game comfortably. My contribution was an undefeated 37 off 68 balls with six fours. Nothing to write home about statistically but it was the first sign that I knew the changes I'd made were starting to pay off. I remember hitting Martin Saggers on the up through the covers and hearing the ball ping sweetly off the bat. I didn't need any of my team-mates to tell me I was hitting the ball well. It felt liberating in a way, like the shackles were off.

We had a couple of second-team friendlies back at Hove. I made 130-odd off about 70 balls against Brighton & Hove and 77 in a Second XI Championship game against Hampshire. I played most of my four-day cricket in the second team that summer and it was great fun, in as much as second-team cricket can be. We had a decent side and Tony

Cottey, the captain, made it as enjoyable as he could. He tried to understand where each of us was in terms of our own development as players, whether it be lads like me trying to get back into the Championship side, or youngsters like Luke Wright, who was just starting to make an impression at Sussex having joined us from Leicestershire at the end of 2003.

Quite often I would only bat in one innings to give some of the other lads an opportunity. I made four half-centuries and had established myself in the one-day side so I was always around the first-team scene. There were setbacks and low scores but I believed in what I was doing because I could see improvements even if they didn't necessarily reflect in my statistics at the time. There was never any thought of going back to my old stance even when I got out cheaply.

Halfway through the summer Cotts got back in the first team when we played Kent at Hove and made a magnificent hundred. A few yards away at the top of the ground Pete Moores had wheeled round the bowling machine from the indoor nets and encouraged me to take guard even further away from leg stump – about a foot and a half in fact – to see if that would be comfortable. It took a while to get used to but once I did I started to feel even more confident. I was hitting it so well all I wanted to do was play or practice, so much so that I had a bit of a disagreement with Pete, who wanted me and Matt Prior to go and do 12th man duties when England asked for two Sussex players to head to Edgbaston to cover the second Test against West Indies. I protested because it meant I would miss a second-team game and another opportunity to get time out in the middle with my new stance. Pete relented and sent Carl Hopkinson instead while I got two half-centuries in a game against Hampshire.

So the batting was going fine. All I needed to do now was make myself a better bowler. It wasn't until 2005 that I switched to left-arm spin. There is a perception about my career that during the winter of 2003/04 I changed both my batting stance and gave up seam bowling but initially I started to bowl little off-cutters off a two- or three-pace run-up. We had a second-team game against The Army where I took a couple of wickets and on the strength of that, and the improvements to my batting, I had got back in the one-day team against Leicestershire at Horsham towards the end of May. I bowled five wicketless overs for 31, which wasn't too bad considering they scored 324 from their 45 overs, before I went in at the end and scored 14 off five balls as we fell one run short of what would have been a wonderful victory.

Towards the end of the season I scored 37 at a run a ball against Somerset at Taunton then made my highest one-day score – 88 off 74 balls – against Derbyshire. That's when the switch went on. That's when it really clicked. I knew that the method I'd worked on for most of that summer was the one I'd have for the rest of my career. No one else in the squad made a big deal about it which was fine. Pete and the coaching staff could see I was happy and more importantly that I was scoring runs now, more consistently and in areas, particularly through the off side and square of the wicket, where I had been a lot less productive in the past. Opposition bowlers initially didn't know what to make of it. There I was scratching my mark a foot and a half outside my leg stump. "Are you ready Yards?" would be the sarcastic cry from the end of the bowler's run-up on more than one occasion. Ready? The truth was I was more ready than I'd ever been.

I got back into the Championship side for our last couple of games. Our title defence had never really got going until the last few weeks when we won five of our final six games to haul ourselves back up the table. We played Middlesex at Hove and scores of 11 and 3 suggested, to the outside world, that not much had changed for me. I wasn't initially selected for the final game of the season against Surrey but Ian Ward dropped out through illness. I was at home pottering about and picked up my phone to find about 20 missed calls and messages urging me to get down to the ground as quickly as possible as Ward's replacement. The wicket was doing a bit and we bowled Surrey out for 283. At stumps on the first day I was 69 not out having opened and seen Richard Montgomerie, Tony Cottey and Murray Goodwin all depart at the other end.

I didn't sleep much that night but I woke up feeling quite relaxed. This was my opportunity and finally, after spending ages in the nineties, I got to three figures and my maiden first-class century. Those last few runs had been a real struggle, despite the constant encouragement I got at the other end from Chris Adams. The over-riding emotion was one of relief, there was certainly no wild celebration because I knew this was a milestone I should have ticked off a lot earlier in my career, not in my fifth season on the staff. Still, I now knew that I had a technique I believed in and one that could enable me to score runs more consistently than before. I was playing shots I'd never played in the past and even Peter Moores, who was always a great enthusiast but was never someone who praised players to the hilt, appeared to be quietly impressed. When he told me at the end of that season that he thought I was hitting the ball in the way he'd expect an overseas batsman to it really struck a chord. Finally, I was away.

I felt so confident that during the winter I even started thinking that if I could push on in 2005 I might get on an England A tour or one of the development squads. Quite a lofty ambition for someone who'd just scored their first Championship hundred but I genuinely believed I was on the verge of becoming a very good player. Yet, at the same time, there was still a little part of me who was worried I might not even start the 2005 season in the Sussex team. Tony Cottey had retired, so a slot was available in the top order, but there were no guarantees.

While I kept my batting ticking over during the winter I worked hard on my bowling and, more specifically, trying to develop myself as a left-arm spinner. Norman Gifford, the former England slow left-armer, lost his job as Sussex coach in 1996 but returned to the county after a spell working with Durham and was always around to help with Sussex's junior squads. I did quite a few sessions with him and Keith Greenfield and in those early days I had quite a nice shape to my action and I could get the ball to spin quite hard. Okay,

I wasn't going to be as effective as someone like Mushtaq Ahmed or even the better finger spinners around at the time but the more I bowled the more I believed I could do a good job as a spin bowler, particularly in one-day cricket. I hadn't bowled spin competitively of course but I guess I was just so settled and confident in my game now that I believed I could go into the new season and get wickets straight away.

In our first pre-season game of 2005 we took on Nottinghamshire at Hove. I played and missed at my first ball but then hit the second from Paul Franks, which was a length delivery outside off stump, for a boundary and I was away. It was as if the 2004 season hadn't ended. Peter Moores had earmarked me for the No.3 spot in the side and when we started the season at The Oval against Surrey I made 111. Suddenly Surrey had become my favourite opponents. The game was ruined by rain and we spent quite a bit of time distracted by a fox which had got stuck on top of one of the famous gas-holders next to the ground. Nearly as important as the century was the wicket I took when I had Jon Batty, who had scored 70 and was playing well, caught at slip by Richard Montgomerie, after he edged a ball that turned quite sharply.

There were practical reasons why I needed to be in the first team. I was still absolutely skint, so much so when Jason Lewry suggested a meal out in London after the second day's play to celebrate my hundred I had to decline. I hadn't eaten at lunch because I'd been batting so I was starving but I couldn't afford to go out. I 'celebrated' with a toasted sandwich at the team hotel. Karin and I had just got a mortgage on a flat in Lancing, which we'd bought after leaving the place in Redhill, and money was very tight. When I started on the staff the team scorer used to give the players their meal expenses in cash in a brown envelope after the second day's play. You would use that for food and drinks, your pocket money for the trip in other words. By 2005 it was being paid into your bank account at the end of the month which was far more efficient for the club's finance department but not much use if you wanted to mark your first hundred of the season with something a bit more exciting than a room-service toastie.

It was during that game that the ECB announced that Peter Moores had been appointed as its next Academy Director, based at Loughborough. We knew Peter would be moving on sooner or later because of the reputation he'd developed as an innovative coach and with Mark Robinson now embedded in the first team alongside him Sussex had their succession plan in place. Knowing Peter would be picking an England A team at the end of the season to tour the West Indies early in 2006 was all the incentive I needed to make sure I kicked on from that hundred at The Oval.

In our first home game I scored 104 against Hampshire and put on 172 with Murray Goodwin, although that match will be remembered for some peppery exchanges on the field between Grizz and Shane Warne, another captain who never knowingly took a step back. Warne and Simon Katich were giving Matt Prior some terrible stick. Warne wanted to get under Matty's skin, presumably because he saw him as a threat, and Ian Gould, the umpire, had to step in a couple of times to calm things down. Kevin Pietersen nearly won the game for them on the final afternoon with a rapid half-century on his Hampshire debut but they lost wickets and shut up shop with 18 runs still needed.

I had scored three centuries in four Championship games and suddenly was starting to attract a bit of national media attention. I made 54 in our next game at Trent Bridge and then a second-innings duck which prompted a last-day collapse and defeat by ten wickets but when we returned to Hove to play Warwickshire I contributed 88 to a stand of 164 with Murray Goodwin as we handed the champions their first defeat in 20 games. I felt so confident that once I'd got to 30 or 40 I believed I would go on and get a really big score, so it was frustrating to fall short. In that regard I learned so much from Murray who, once he'd got himself in, invariably went big. He was a remorseless accumulator once he'd got his eye in and the measure of the opposition bowlers.

I felt I needed to really cash in on my form so I was always going to play against the touring Bangladeshis when they arrived at Hove three days later, even though I would have been rested if I'd asked. The pitch was flat, their attack fairly modest and I made hay with 257, batting just shy of seven hours to compile the highest score by a Sussex batsman against a touring team and hitting 35 fours and two sixes. I think I gave one chance when I should have been stumped on 218 but other than that I never felt in any trouble. I didn't think there was a delivery they could bowl that would get me out, a state of mind that happened only a handful of times in my career. I would hit anything there to be hit, block when I had to do and leave when I had to. Simple really. If only it had been like that all the time.

The bonus for me in that game was that as well as my career-best with the bat I more than doubled my tally of first-class wickets by taking 5 for 83 as we won the match. Because I was making such a big contribution to the team now with the bat I felt much less pressure when I bowled. It was coming out nicely and I was finally starting to develop a reputation as a bit of a golden arm. I got a couple of wickets in a rain-affected Championship draw against Glamorgan at Swansea, including the Australian opening batsman Matthew Elliott, and after bowling only a single over in limited overs cricket in the first two months of the season I started to make an impact with the white ball as well.

A couple of matches stick out. We'd got on a roll in the Totesport one-day league second division and when we played Somerset at Hove in early August I took 4 for 26, then my best figures in limited-overs cricket. A couple of weeks later we played Warwickshire at Edgbaston and I ended up with 6 for 27 on a dry wicket which turned quite a lot. Both games were televised by Sky Sports and for the first time some of their commentators, particularly the former England coach David Lloyd, started to mention me as a possible future England candidate. Ask any player. If you want to impress, make sure you do it in front of the TV cameras. England selectors definitely took more notice of performances they saw for themselves, even if it was on the box. It's still the case now and no doubt always will be.

After my double hundred against Bangladesh I experienced a dip in form. There was real pressure on me now to perform. I considered myself the next most reliable batsman in the team behind Murray Goodwin and with that came expectation from my team-mates and the Sussex supporters to score consistently. I got my form back with 106 against Gloucestershire and then 179 in one of the most extraordinary games I ever played in against Middlesex at Lord's. We won the toss and found it tough initially, but at 199 for 6 I was joined by our new overseas player Rana Naved.

Rana proved to be an outstanding foil for Mushtaq, who had recommended him to Sussex, with the ball. He could reverse it at will – a skill he passed on to Jason Lewry who probably enjoyed an extra two years at the end of his career as a result of having this extra weapon in his armoury. When he got his eye in Rana was a fearsome ball-striker. We smashed 230 runs between lunch and tea and another 198 before the close. There was a short boundary on the Tavern side and I remember Rana should have been caught on the rope when he'd scored 69 but we ended up hammering 522 runs in a day, the most scored by any team on the opening day of a Championship match for 20 years. Rana finished with a career-best 139 at the home of cricket, an innings he was still talking about when he came back to Sussex for a second spell a few years later, complete with a luxuriant hair transplant. That day at Lord's it was like taking runs off a village attack at times. Middlesex were totally demoralised and we bowled them out cheaply twice to win inside two days and briefly went back to the top of the Championship table.

Unfortunately, we still had to play Warwickshire at Edgbaston, a ground where we hadn't won since 1982, and duly capitulated on the last day when we were only chasing 228. There was bad blood between the teams too. Their coaching staff secretly filmed James Kirtley bowling during their first innings and sent the footage to Lord's. James had already remodelled his action once in his career and as a result of what happened in Birmingham he had to go through it again that winter. So we finished third in the Championship and my personal contribution was 1,217 runs at an average of 48.18. At least on the last day of the season we won promotion to the first division of the Totesport League after beating Yorkshire to give Peter Moores the send-off he deserved.

Not long after the season finished my old county coach was in touch again. My performances had earned me my first England call-up for the A tour to West Indies in early 2006. Before Christmas I had to go to Loughborough with the rest of the Academy squad for practice and preparation. Having got married in the French village where Karin's parents lived and then had our honeymoon I had permission from Pete to turn up at Loughborough a few days late.

It was unavoidable but not ideal and as soon as I arrived at the performance centre I had a bit of an inferiority complex. I didn't feel I belonged in such exalted company. My revamped batting technique had got me there in the first place but now, when I compared myself to the likes of Rob Key, Ed Joyce, Owais Shah and even a young left-hander from Essex who everyone was raving about called Alastair Cook, I felt frankly inadequate. They were all wonderful players and didn't need my strange trigger movements to hit the ball as sweet as a nut.

Coming to terms with this step up was hard enough. Playing for the full England team was certainly not on my radar. During the summer of 2005, like the rest of the country, I'd been gripped by the Ashes series when we finally won back the urn after five fantastic Test matches. Even Karin, who'd shown very little interest in cricket before then, was hooked. Then in late November I got a phone call from Matt Prior, who was with the England one-day squad in Pakistan. The captain, Michael Vaughan, had come home, after Pakistan had punctured England's post-Ashes optimism by winning the Test series 2-0, to have surgery on his knee and the coach, Duncan Fletcher, had spoken to Matt at length about my qualities. In the end, Ian Blackwell played in all five one-day internationals. Even though I didn't think I was in England's plans I clearly was. I'd never met Duncan or talked to him on the phone. In fact, the first conversation we had was when I did finally make my international debut in August 2006.

The England A squad that went to the West Indies was very strong. Before we left Pete Moores told us that he thought its sole purpose was to prepare us for the senior international side but I don't expect even he imagined it would happen as quickly as it did. On the first day of the opening 'Test' match against West Indies A in St John's Antigua we lost both Alastair Cook and James Anderson to the Test team in India and two days later Owais Shah followed them. Then, as soon as the one-dayers were over the captain, Vikram Solanki, along with Kabir Ali, Gareth Batty and Sajid Mahmood, all went off to join the senior limited-overs squad.

Nine of the West Indies team had international experience and the two Tests were closely fought. We lost the first by one wicket and drew the second. I opened with Ed Joyce in both but didn't do well with scores of 16, 0, 9 and 0. The cricket was very competitive but off the field it was all a bit village. We got to St Lucia for the second Test and found the groundsman painting the black sightscreens white because he'd only just been told that morning it was a four-day game. And when we went into lunch on the first day there was no food because it hadn't been ordered.

I felt a bit more settled during the one-day series, which we lost 3-2. After getting a fifth-ball duck in the opening game I was dropped but returned for the third match and made 12 and bowled four wicketless overs for 22. Then, in the fourth match in Barbados, I removed Darren Sammy for my first international wicket and in the decider I got Carlton Baugh out and scored 28 batting at No.5, having batted at No. 3 in the fourth match. I enjoyed the tour. I got to know quite a few of the lads I'd later play alongside during my England career and I had taken another step up the ladder, albeit a somewhat faltering one.

Karin joined me for the last week of the tour and we stayed on for a holiday but after the struggle I'd had to adapt to international cricket if you'd told me that in less than six months I would be making my full England debut I would probably have thought you'd been enjoying too many of the special 'cigarettes' the local guys would try and sell us on the Caribbean beaches.

When the 2006 domestic season started I had a bit to prove. I was a senior player now and needed to start well, especially if I was to maintain the interest of the England selectors. In our opening home Championship game we played Warwickshire and despite scoring 48 we conceded a first-innings deficit of 147. We were 32 for 2 in our second innings when I was joined by Murray Goodwin and we proceeded to bat through the rest of the third day and the entire final day, putting on 385 for the third wicket – the second-highest stand for any wicket in Sussex's history. The pitch had flattened out but I played really well for my 159 and having Murray at the other end was always a pleasurable experience for me when I batted. I'm sure there were a lot of players on the circuit who thought my achievements in 2005 were a bit freakish – a one-off – but Murray believed in me and my ability. He would offer me tips if I was struggling to play a certain type of bowling, particularly spinners, because he knew I was capable of following his advice. For instance, if a slow bowler was getting lots of turn out of the rough he'd tell me to use my feet or sweep hard. He knew I could execute the shot, I just needed a little direction sometimes.

What a summer it turned out to be. We won the Championship again, triumphed at Lord's in the final of the

Cheltenham & Gloucester Trophy and really should have celebrated the treble. We needed to win our final game against Nottinghamshire in the Pro40 League and also hope that Essex lost but we got rolled for 110 and were beaten easily. A few days later, though, we were spraying champagne all over the Trent Bridge outfield after winning our second Championship title in three years.

Mushy finished with 102 wickets and Jason Lewry and Robin Martin-Jenkins took up the slack with James Kirtley reduced to seven Championship appearances as he grooved his remodelled action. Those two took 98 wickets between them and Rana Naved 35 in just six appearances in the first half of the season before he was replaced by Yasir Arafat, although Rana did return for the finale against Nottinghamshire. With the bat, Murray finished with 1,649 Championship runs and the captain 1,218. I ended up with 914 at 50.77 from 12 games, my appearances having been restricted by my England call-up in August.

We won six of our first eight matches – Sussex's best start to a Championship season since 1934 – and although it took us until the final game to wrap up the title I never thought we would be caught.

We had a core of ten players, six of whom played in 15 or all of the 16 games, plus Matt Prior and Robin Martin-Jenkins, who only missed two matches, myself and Luke Wright, who played in ten of them. In the finale against Nottinghamshire I came back into the team full of confidence after a promising England debut and made my third hundred of the season (119) having also scored 159 against Kent earlier in the summer.

As so often happens if you get momentum in one format it spills over into another. We won six of our first seven games in the Cheltenham & Gloucester Trophy, which had been split into two all-play north and south groups with the winners contesting the final at Lord's. Hampshire kept pace with us and the meeting at Hove on 16 June effectively became a knockout semi-final. Mushy and I bowled well together to take a combined 2 for 61 from 20 overs after they had threatened to score a total of around 300. We restricted them to 254 and a rejuvenated James Kirtley finished with 5 for 43. James had worked hard for months on his new action and this was the first time it had paid dividends. What's more it came against the side who had needed little encouragement in previous meetings to voice their doubts about the legality of it.

Even that day Shane Warne, Nic Pothas and Shaun Udal couldn't resist having a go at him. We were furious and I told Pothas, their wicketkeeper, that he was out of order. "How the fuck can you sit in judgement on someone's career?" was the gist of my argument. It was only when James hit the stumps three times in his final over that they finally shut up. Nic joined Sussex's coaching staff for my last season in 2015 and I really enjoyed working with him and reminiscing about past battles on the pitch. I can see him having a good career in coaching, possibly even at international level.

When we batted Carl Hopkinson made 69 and I contributed 41 to a match-winning stand as we won with an over to spare. Hampshire didn't take defeat well. Dominic Thornely mis-fielded on the boundary when Hoppo and I were batting together and threw his cap into the crowd after he got some good-natured abuse which we all found hilarious. That's when we knew we were going to Lord's. We'd enjoyed the new format mainly because splitting the counties geographically meant less travelling, although we did have to make one long trip to Dublin to play Ireland. The down side was that it was two months between the end of the group stages and the final against Lancashire on 26 August. Plenty of time to lose that momentum we'd built up.

It was Sussex's first Lord's final since the infamous game in 1993 when they had lost to Warwickshire after making 321 for 6 and for a lot of the guys their first experience of a big game – myself included. That can be the only explanation for the nerves which seemed to afflict us early on after Lancashire had put us in under sullen early-autumn skies. When Carl Hopkinson was run out for 1 we were 52 for 5 and then 78 for 6 when Yasir Arafat came in to join me and slowly we began to cobble together a partnership.

Subsequently, when I was asked which was my favourite innings for Sussex, I always nominated this one. In truth, it wasn't a thing of beauty as my stats – 37 runs off 120 balls with one four nicked through the slips – would indicate. I had to fight and scrap for every run, eschewing all risk, because I knew that if either Yasir or I got out we'd have no chance of setting Lancashire any sort of target. We took the score to 134 for 7 and eventually finished with 172. Probably not enough, but at least it was something to defend. Throughout the latter stages of our innings I sensed Lancashire's growing confidence and when we gathered in the dressing room during the interval I got, shall we say, a bit emotional.

"They're taking the fucking piss out of us, they are taking the fucking piss!"

I must have repeated those words a dozen times. A few of the lads were surprised at my outburst. Matt Prior later admitted he found it hard to stop giggling he was so amused. In the end, Mark Robinson had to calm me down so he could do the 'proper' team talk so to speak. There was still a bit in the wicket and when James Kirtley struck three times in his first spell to remove Mal Loye, Nathan Astle and Stuart Law, who always got big runs against us but this time made a duck, we knew we were in business.

Mushy bowled brilliantly as his figures of 2 for 19 from ten overs will attest. Luke Wright, who could bowl a heavy ball back then, and I did a decent fill-in job but this was Kirtley's day. When he removed Murali Kartik to complete his five-for – all leg before wicket for only the third time in the history of one-day cricket – he couldn't hide his emotion anymore. He sank to his knees and moments later was engulfed by the rest of us.

All the hard work, the hours spent in the nets at Hove the previous winter working on his remodelled action, had finally paid off. It wasn't classic Kirtley firing in yorkers and slower balls all the time. It was holding length and bowling with a good, high action. After all he'd been through each and every one of us was both delighted and proud of what he – and the team – had achieved. He had been on a tough journey and if there was ever a message that desire and commitment could succeed then this was it.

We celebrated our first Lord's victory since 1986 long into the night. Well, ten of the team and the support staff did. I had a nice meal and a couple of beers before slipping off to bed. While the rest of the lads were getting on a coach and travelling to Durham the next day to play a one-day game on Bank Holiday Monday, I was heading in a completely different direction.

Down the M4 in fact – to begin my England career.

6

England

ON the pitch, batting or bowling or in the outfield, haring round the boundary trying to stop the ball or running in hard from mid-wicket or the covers and shying at the stumps.

That was the best part about playing for England.

I know I should have embraced the rest of it – being around the best cricketers in the country, travelling to some fantastic places, taking on the world's best players and getting paid pretty well for it too.

And I really wish I had at the time because it might have helped me deal with the issues relating to my mental health that I kept ignoring before I made my tearful exit from the 2011 World Cup.

I used to love getting a good sweat on in the gym, but with England I didn't enjoy training as much. I enjoyed the batting and bowling but was very aware I had to continually work at my fielding.

Look, I know I was very privileged. I played 42 games for my country. Hundreds of cricketers over the years would have given their right arm to wear the England shirt just once. And I am one of just 11 Englishmen, at the time of writing, to have won a world championship. Helping England triumph in the T20 World Cup in the West Indies in 2010 was one of the highlights of my career. Just one of the highlights you might be asking? Well yes, I would rank leading Sussex to the domestic T20 title in 2009 in my first season as captain of the county alongside it in terms of career achievements.

I wish I could have enjoyed it more, relished it even. I really do. I thought I held my own in T20 cricket and my stats back that up. I wish there had been more T20 internationals to play during my five years in and out of the England side but during the last decade the most there were during a non-World Cup year were one or two tacked onto the end of a one-day series, almost as an afterthought.

The problem for me was the 50-over format. I could say with some justification that I was never given a regular role in the team with the bat, shunted up and down the order as I was. I played 28 one-day internationals and batted in every position from No.3 to No.8. But the harsh reality is I wasn't good enough in the longer format. I did make some runs but not consistently enough and although I was confident I could keep batsmen tied down for four overs in T20 I found it was a lot harder bowling eight or ten overs in a one-day international. It was no surprise that I was normally the bowler the opposition targeted and sometimes I struggled to find the right response.

Initially, though, it was a real thrill. When I was told by Mark Robinson after nets at Hove that I'd been selected for the one-day series, which was to be preceded by two T20 internationals, against Pakistan in August 2006 I was delighted. It didn't come as a huge surprise though. I'd had a good domestic season and with one or two injuries about the coach, Duncan Fletcher, decided to give me an opportunity. They had tried Warwickshire off-spinner Alex Loudon and Ian Blackwell, of Somerset and later Durham, with limited success and there weren't too many other options in terms of a spinning all-rounder.

What did seem a bit odd was that I was in the England squad just two years after I played my first T20 game for Sussex. When the competition started in 2003 I wasn't in the team but watching matches at Hove in those early weeks certainly whetted my appetite. I remember I couldn't get the car into the ground for one game because there were so many spectators queueing down Eaton Road trying to get in. Suddenly friends who had no real interest in cricket apart from checking how I was doing were after tickets and everyone wanted to play in the games.

Players who were on the fringes of the one-day side, such as myself, suddenly had this massive incentive because we could all see how enjoyable it was, not least the experience of playing in front of a big crowd which was not something we were used to apart from the odd one-day game when there might be 3,000 at Hove. Looking back 13 years later, you have to wonder why it took us so long to come up with T20 cricket. In a lot of ways it probably saved English domestic cricket as we know it. Towards the end of my career with Sussex, most of the chat among the lads at the start of each season was about who was going to get into the T20 team. When I started, it was all about finding a route into the Championship side.

I was told on the Monday before the Cheltenham & Gloucester Trophy final against Lancashire about my England selection. It certainly made me less nervous ahead of the Lord's Final. All of a sudden I had to think about how I was going to combat Shoaib Akhtar, 90mph of wild-haired fast-bowling menace, or get some great players of spin out. Better get the bowling machine out and crank up the speed dial.

Before the Lord's final we played a couple of T20s against Essex, home and away, in a one-off competition arranged before the season had started to cash in on the popularity of the format. It was odd preparation for the 50-over final and it seems strange looking back a decade later that I wasn't wrapped in cotton wool by England ahead of that game and a possible debut. But I played in both without giving it a second thought and it was actually useful practice.

While the other lads partied hard after we beat Lancashire I slipped away from the revelry fairly early. I'd been excused England practice on the Sunday before the first T20 international on Bank Holiday Monday but at the team meeting after I'd driven down from London Duncan took me aside, congratulated me on making the squad and told me I would be playing the next day.

Having had two very productive domestic seasons, particularly in the Championship, I definitely saw my promotion to the one-day squad as a possible route into the England Test team and a lot of guys I played with then went on to have very good Test careers. I had spoken to Matt Prior about what to expect but I was left pretty much to my own devices in terms of preparation. Of course there were nets with the rest of the squad but you also had the opportunity to work on your game with the coaches on a one-on-one basis as well. Then you would come together as a team for pre-match meetings. All of this was totally alien to me. County cricket was completely the opposite. In that environment it's team, team, team and when I became Sussex captain in 2009 I tried to change our ethos a little so that the players took a bit more responsibility for their own game.

There were 14,511 people inside the County Ground at Bristol to see me make my England debut. Hard to believe now, but it was only the eighth T20 international that had ever been played. Marcus Trescothick made 53 but we lost three wickets in five balls early on and could only cobble together 144 for 7, which included an unbeaten 24 from me batting at No.8. My first international wicket – Mohammad Yousuf – wasn't a bad one and I was pleased with my figures of 1 for 20 from three overs. But Pakistan won by five wickets with

13 balls to spare after Shahid Afridi smashed 28 off 10 balls. I took a catch in the deep to end his innings off Middlesex's left-arm spinner Jamie Dalrymple that I was particularly proud of as the ball swirled in the air for ages before I clung onto it on the boundary edge. So far, so good.

I didn't play under Andrew Strauss too often but his captaincy impressed me. He wasn't big on chest-thumping rhetoric but he planned meticulously. He had a good relationship with Duncan Fletcher, but for me there's no doubt he did his best work with Andy Flower. They might not have agreed on everything, but they always presented a united front with the players and I felt that was important.

I wasn't picked for the first three games of the one-day series and by the time we got to Trent Bridge for the fourth game on 8 September – a day-night match – Pakistan were 2-0 up. But we won by eight wickets, the first victory England had enjoyed in an ODI in 2006. I had a really good game. I picked up 3 for 24 from my ten overs including my bunny Yousuf for the second time as well as Shoaib Malik and their feisty little wicketkeeper Kamran Akmal. *Wisden* weren't too complimentary about my action: 'Yardy bowled quick and flat left-arm spin reminiscent of a darts player peppering the treble 20' but I enjoyed the experience in front of an appreciative full house. Who wouldn't?

I'd been with the squad for a fortnight but had still barely had a proper conversation with Duncan. I remember before the game at Lord's I was having a bowl-through in the middle and he must have stood behind the stumps watching me for about 35 minutes. He didn't say a word in all that time which I found quite unnerving. What was he looking for? I had become used to coaches who would stop you now and then and make suggestions or offer a word of encouragement on the way you were playing. I didn't really have what I would call a proper conversation with Duncan until early in 2007 when I was in India with the Champions Trophy squad. We were all appraised before the game against Australia in Jaipur and I went in expecting a review of how I'd done since I came into the England set-up. Instead, all we talked about was making sure I was aware that all the Australians, even the bowlers like Brett Lee and Nathan Bracken, had gun arms and I had to be alert to that when I went in to bat. He didn't mention how to bowl to Adam Gilchrist or Ricky Ponting or what was the best way to combat Glenn McGrath. I guess I had to figure that out for myself.

That was Duncan in a nutshell really. Attention to detail was his forte and occasionally he'd come up with a random idea which made people sit up. He once asked if we'd considered shining the white ball on both sides. There were a lot of puzzled looks. Surely he knew we only shined it on one side to make it swing? Matt Maynard, his assistant, was a lot more gregarious and a better communicator. They worked well as a partnership and I know there are a lot of guys who played for England at that time who benefitted from the little tweaks to their game that Duncan had suggested, especially when facing quality spin bowlers. I guess, quite rightly, he reasoned that players he had brought into that environment didn't need a lot of work. That's why they were international players, because their skills were high class and could be delivered under pressure on a consistent basis.

My problem was a lack of self belief. The hardest thing I found to accept was being outperformed by an opponent. It was hard for me to reconcile with the fact that on some days the man at the other end was better than me. When I didn't play well I tended to think it was because I'd bowled poorly or played the wrong shot, not because my opponent had been too good for me. When someone collared my bowling or made me look like a novice with the bat I took it personally.

I wish I could have had more self-belief. Even someone like KP accepted on the odd occasion he was outplayed by an opponent. It didn't happen very often but sometimes he'd come off after getting out cheaply and praise the bowler to the hilt. I remember him eulogising about Mohammad Asif during that Pakistan series in 2006. The difference between his thought process and mine was that Kevin regarded anyone who got him out a few times as some sort of cricketing Superman. He had that thick skin which I think the very best players have.

I got on okay with KP. He was a huge factor in our success in the World T20 in 2010, a tournament he came into despite having had a poor season in the Indian Premier League. Kevin didn't contribute massively to team meetings but I do remember one amusing moment before we played Sri Lanka during the tournament. The captain, Paul Collingwood, tried to keep those briefings short and sharp and was just winding things up when KP put his hand up and stared at me. "Yards, look. Mahela (Jayawardene) is going to target you today and you'd better be ready. He's going to come after you hard." I think it was the only time during my England career that a team-mate said something like that. It was difficult for me to stop myself laughing and I think the other lads felt the same. Colly interjected. "With all due respect Kev, Yards has bowled pretty well in the tournament and I'm sure he'll find a way." Jayawardene got out early on and I didn't have to bowl to him anyway, but thanks for the advice Kevin!

Back to 2006 and we won the final one-day match at Edgbaston to square the series. I got Kamran Akmal out again and hit the winning runs with 19 overs to go. I had enjoyed my first taste of international cricket and was delighted when I was chosen to go to India for the Champions Trophy in early 2007. With games against India, Australia and West Indies it was a big step up but one I was looking forward to, especially as there was a World Cup to come a few months later for which I was definitely in the frame for selection. There was a new captain too in Andrew Flintoff and although it was only a brief experience for me I enjoyed playing under Fred. I admired what he'd achieved, particularly during the 2005 Ashes, as a player and I guess like quite a few of the England lads I was a little bit in awe of him. I liked that he always gave everything he had, even if it didn't always come off. He was someone who you wanted to go out and bust a gut for.

I got through the India trip okay. I wasn't homesick but I found it tough to amuse myself between games. We played

India in Jaipur and it was another six days before the next
fixture against Australia. We then had a week to wait before
taking on West Indies in Ahmedabad. We were cooped up in
the hotel for a lot of the time and I found that uncomfortable,
the first signs of the problems I would experience a few years
later. Fortunately, Steve Harmison had virtually turned his
room into the saloon bar of his local pub, without the alcohol
of course. He put a darts board up on the wall and managed to
stream all the Premier League football from England onto his
laptop. I spent more time in his room than mine on that trip
and we got on famously. I loved his openness and honesty. I
never walked away from a conversation with him wondering
'is that what he really thinks of me?'

The wickets weren't great and after losing to India and
Australia we beat West Indies, but we were knocked out at the
group stage. I batted at four against India and then dropped
down a place for both of the other games. Initially, I thought
they had earmarked me for No.7 so when Freddie knocked
on my door before the India game and told me I was going in
at four it came as a complete surprise. They reasoned that I
would be a good bloke to have between him at three and KP at
five. Did I think I was good enough to bat at No.4 for England
in an ODI? Absolutely not. But the more I thought about
it the more I felt it was actually quite a sensible suggestion.
Unfortunately, it was not a success. I made 4 runs at four, 4 at
five and 10 at six but I didn't have much luck either. Against
India I was bowled off an inside edge, in the Australia game I
was caught off my shirt flap down the leg side and caught at

long off against West Indies. The wickets weren't conducive to spin but I bowled with a good economy rate of 2.9 but when the World Cup squad was chosen the selectors chose Monty Panesar and Jamie Dalrymple as the slow-bowling options. I felt a little hard done by.

When I returned to the England team on a regular basis in 2010 I thought I was good enough to bat in the top six. But I was stuck in the lower middle-order by then and although we still weren't a good one-day side I knew that guys like Ravi Bopara and Paul Collingwood would always be chosen ahead of me at five or six. Perhaps if I'd had more self-belief things might have been different but I was still battling myself and questioning whether I was good enough to compete at this level.

The consolation for me was the captaincy of the England A team in March 2007. Matt Prior and James Kirtley, my Sussex team-mates, also made the trip which was thoroughly enjoyable. In tough conditions we won the one-day series 2-1 and while we were there Sussex announced that I would become Chris Adams' vice-captain at Sussex. Grizzly was about to start his tenth season in charge and this was the next step for me in becoming his successor.

Back in England I knew I needed to start the 2007 domestic season well and I did. I was on 99 in the annual curtain-raiser between the champion county and MCC at Lord's and batting well against a strong attack led by Steve Harmison and including Matthew Hoggard, Graham Onions and Adil Rashid. Matt Prior had just come in to bat during a really quick spell by Harmison and started swinging from the hip, a tactic Harmy wasn't enamoured with. I remember ducking under a bouncer and turning to square leg where Alex Loudon was fielding and I knew what he was thinking: "Rather you than me Yards." The next ball I defended on my toes as it hit my glove. I felt a pins and needles sensation in the index finger of my left hand and at the end of the over, when I took my glove off, Matt had to turn away because it looked so bad. I glanced down and the top half of my finger was literally hanging off. I went to hospital and had a metal plate inserted and was ruled out for seven weeks. It was the worst injury of my career simply because of the timing of it.

If I was going to achieve my ambition of making the Test team I knew this was the season where I had to make that move, to churn out runs with even more consistency than I had in 2005 and 2006 in the County Championship. A score of 99 not out against a quality attack was a great start but now I was left kicking my heels. When I did get back I spent the rest of the season catching up and getting more and more frustrated.

I made my comeback against Lancashire in a four-day game at the end of May and swept my second ball from Muttiah Muralitharan for four. Few shots during my career felt so good and my mood improved further when Sajid Mahmood struck me on the finger that had been broken and all seemed fine. But then, when I was on 42 and playing well, Murali got an outrageously bad lbw decision against me with a ball that pitched a foot outside leg stump. I was mightily pissed off and let it affect me and not just for the rest of that game. It was another five weeks before I scored my first half-century of the season. I wasn't relaxed, my triggers didn't seem to be as effective and trying to force things just made it even worse. I finally got going again with a hundred against Sri Lanka A in July and made my only Championship century against Yorkshire in early September as I finished the summer quite strongly.

Yet despite my struggles I was still on England's radar which gave me a massive shot in the arm when I was at a pretty low ebb. I played against West Indies for the newly renamed England Lions at New Road in Worcester and whilst I was there Peter Moores, who had just succeeded Duncan Fletcher as England coach, sounded me out. "So, if Chris Gayle smashes the ball back at the finger you broke you're catching it right?" Of course I was. At the end of June I played in two T20 internationals against West Indies at The Oval and a few days later in the one-dayer at Edgbaston. That turned out to be my last England appearance for nearly three years. My performances were steady enough and there was a nice moment when Matt Prior got a stumping off my bowling down the leg side to remove Dwayne Bravo. I can't honestly say it was something we'd been working on since playing together for Sussex under-12s but it was a great personal moment nonetheless. Two lads who had played junior cricket together teaming up for their country.

While I was still on the fringes of the England set-up Matt had taken to international cricket as to the manor born. I'll never forget watching him score a hundred on Test debut against West Indies at Lord's. Sussex were playing Surrey in a Championship game at Hove but as Matt moved through the gears the spectators started drifting inside to watch the Test match on TV. When he got to three figures there was a roar from inside the pavilion so loud that the game was temporarily stopped as the players looked across and wondered what all the fuss was about. The number of people actually watching the match when it happened was just about in double figures.

I was thrilled for Matt. I always realised he was more talented than me, although you never know just how good someone will be early in their career. Matt's an all or nothing person so when the runs became more difficult to score and scrutiny increased on his wicketkeeping his response was exactly what I anticipated. If he knew he had to work hard to achieve something that's what Matt would do. Bruce French, the former England and Nottinghamshire wicketkeeper, became something of a mentor for him and they would team up on many occasions at Hove. Eventually, Matt turned himself into the best keeper-batsman in the world and became an integral part of the side which won three successive Ashes series between 2009 and 2013. I believe that there are quite a few England players who could have had careers similar to his if they'd had Matt's strength of mind. I'm proud of the fact that when I played for England I never left anything on the pitch. Matt was exactly the same.

7

Top of the world

IF I always harboured doubts about my ability to make a telling contribution for England in one-day internationals, I had no such reservations when it came to T20 and by the time I was recalled in 2010 I felt I was one of the best English players in the format.

The previous year I'd led Sussex to their first domestic T20 title. I was proud not only of the way I had captained the side but also of my own contribution, particularly with the ball. That year I took 13 wickets and in 11 of the 13 games I played I conceded 30 runs or fewer in my four-over spell. We had such a strong line-up of stroke players that I was rarely needed to bat.

But when Andy Flower called to tell me I was going to the World Cup I was a bit taken aback. Not many players return to the international fold after a three-year break, especially players like me who hadn't exactly set the world alight first time around. I'd had a great first season as captain of Sussex, had come through some difficult times off the pitch and I was very comfortable personally and in terms of my career at the end of 2009. I'd almost forgotten about England if I'm honest. I was still ambitious but I was also realistic. Playing for my country again was not at the forefront of my mind, I hadn't chased it or expected it. So when I was selected I made a vow. This time I would try and enjoy every aspect of the whole England experience – not just what happened on the pitch.

It helped that the tournament was in the West Indies. I'd always enjoyed playing in the Caribbean so I knew that there was less likelihood of being confined to my hotel room all the time. Not only was it a fun place to play but you could enjoy yourself off the field there as well without too much hassle. And as soon as the squad got together, I had a little feeling we might surprise a few people in the tournament itself.

Andy Flower was the third England coach I worked with and it was always a pleasure to play for him. Paul Collingwood had been appointed one-day captain and the pair of them clicked straight away. The emphasis was on enjoyment and playing without any fear and Colly always came across as relaxed and in control. In terms of selection we'd finally caught up with other countries as well. Michael Lumb and Craig Kieswetter had done very well domestically and were a potentially explosive opening pair of power hitters, we had Kevin Pietersen with a point to prove after he'd struggled a

My first Sussex pre-season photo call in 2000. Nice fringe!

By 2001 I'd gone for a spikier hairstyle

Short back and sides for 2002. I look like a raw recruit to the Army!

My first England tour to the Champions Trophy in early 2007

I was surprised to get an England recall in the summer of 2007. Here I am scoring an unbeaten 23 against West Indies at The Oval in a T20 international

My proudest moment with Sussex when we won the T20 and did a one-day double in 2009

Jumping for joy against South Africa during the 2010 World Cup when I dismissed Robin Peterson

Brad Haddin admires my sweep shot during a one-day international against Australia in Sydney in 2011

Celebrating with Steven Finn after I took a catch off his bowling against Australia in Sydney early in 2011

One of my last practice sessions with England in 2011. I was ready to come home and face up to my struggle with depression

Yasir Arafat and I put on some vital runs in the 2006 Cheltenham & Gloucester Final at Lord's

We didn't do ourselves justice in the 2009 Cheltenham & Gloucester Trophy Final against Hampshire

In the Hove nets in 2008. Not a pretty look!

A nice moment as the Yorkshire players shake my hand after my final innings for Sussex in September 2015

Take a bow, son. A hundred in my final game for Sussex at Hove against Somerset

My first England man of the match award against Pakistan in 2010. A couple of weeks later I'd quit the squad in tears

Working with Duncan Fletcher in 2006. He was a man of few words but I admired him as a coach

Leaving the field at Hove for the last time – a very emotional moment

Murray Goodwin taught me to sweep hard. By 2015, when I hit this shot for four against Yorkshire at Hove, I think I'd cracked it!

One of my first photo-shoots as captain, promoting cancer awareness

Sharing a joke with Luke Wright at press day in 2010. Mark Robinson doesn't seem amused though!

Captain of Sussex. At the formal announcement in 2009

Magical moment. Celebrating my first hundred against Surrey in 2004

Syenna, Marley and Raffy

On holiday with the kids in France in 2015

The kids help me clear out my locker at Hove for the last time

He was born in Worthing, but Raffy was always going to be a West Ham fan like me!

A recent gathering of the Yardy family

Raffy and Syenna after the Hove Park fun run

My rock. Karin and I on our wedding day

High five from Raffy on my last day at Hove

Guard of honour from the kids after my last game for Sussex

bit prior to the tournament in the Indian Premier League and Eoin Morgan, who was just beginning to emerge as a world-class batsman. He was still relatively young then but he was absolutely fearless and technically strong. I regarded him as good a player as KP at that time and since then he's got better and better. He'd be in my fantasy world T20 team every time.

There was good variety in the bowling attack too with Ryan Sidebottom the left-arm option to back up Stuart Broad and Tim Bresnan. I shared the spin-bowling duties with Graeme Swann who, at the time, was arguably the best finger spinner in the world and a great team man who would always say something amusing to lighten the mood. Luke Wright helped to balance the side and, with Colly's medium pace, gave us seven different bowling options in case anyone had a bad day. With Luke coming in at No.6 and Bresnan, who also hit a long ball, at No.7, we had some batting depth too. I felt, if necessary, that I could perform a role with the bat but the management also recognised that I was a very experienced bowler in the format by then and they wanted to utilise that knowledge.

I was put in charge of the Duckworth/Lewis calculations sheet for each match to make sure there were no fuck-ups if there was rain about. It doesn't seem like much of a responsibility but that small gesture made me feel great and I came away from the meeting where they told me feeling ten foot tall. For the first time in my England career I really felt valued by the team management.

We won our two warm-up games against Bangladesh and South Africa and I was sitting down in a bar after the South Africa game with Luke Wright and Stuart Broad, who was effectively keeping James Anderson out of the team, which showed how strong we were. "I think we've got a serious chance here," Broad said. We had come into the tournament with little expectation other than that we had for ourselves but everyone in the squad got on while Collingwood and Flower were like a breath of fresh air.

Yet we nearly didn't make it to the Super 8s. We lost our first game against West Indies in Guyana by eight wickets, a farcical match ruined by Duckworth/Lewis. We made 191 for 8 and they were 30 for 0 from 14 deliveries when it started to rain. When we got back out the D/L calculation was 60 off six overs and with wickets in hand they could afford to smash it. I caught Chris Gayle off Graeme Swann and the ball hit me so hard that next day I woke up with a plate-sized bruise on my chest but they got the runs with a ball to spare.

That left us having to beat Ireland the next day and this time we were grateful when the heavens suddenly opened. The pitch was terrible. It must have been about the tenth day running it had been used – slow, low and with big cracks – and their seamers intelligently took pace off the ball and restricted us to 120 for 8. Eoin Morgan made 45 off 37 balls, a masterclass in those conditions, and Ireland were 14 for 1 in the fourth over when it hosed it down. Fortunately for us, West Indies had already beaten Ireland so we progressed because of our superior net run rate but it had been mighty close. My tournament, it could be fairly said, had started quietly. One over for six runs against West Indies, the catch off Gayle and two did not bats.

We left Guyana to return to Barbados feeling immensely relieved and immediately felt more settled. There was more to do away from practice and matches, there were plenty of English supporters on the island and the Kensington Oval was a ground we enjoyed playing at. In our first game of the Super 8s Kevin Pietersen led us to victory with an unbeaten 73 after we'd restricted Pakistan to 147 for 9. I took 2 for 19 and between us, Swann and I finished with 3 for 47 from our eight overs. The pitch had some bounce which helped the pair of us, particularly Swanny who was always looking to attack.

When we played in St Lucia against New Zealand there was a short leg-side boundary and I assumed I'd be bowling at that end. Swanny over-ruled me because that's where the breeze was coming from and he thought it gave him a better chance of getting batsmen out. I think that mentality is a common denominator with all the world-class spinners when you think of wonderful bowlers like Shane Warne, Muttiah Muralitharan and Anil Kumble from the last couple of decades. At his best, Swanny was as good as them and to a certain extent, even though our roles in the team were different, it rubbed off on me. There was a short boundary at the Kensington Oval as well which it was my job to protect but when Swanny took a wicket he always saw it as his best chance to attack. He'd bring an extra man in, put pressure on the batsmen and even make his opponent think there was more in the wicket than there really was. We dovetailed well. It was an odd combination – I think someone in the press nicknamed us the odd couple – but for those three weeks in 2010 it worked.

Colly would consult with me quite regularly during the games and that was massive for my own confidence. Every time I went out onto the pitch I felt good. As a player at international level, I don't think you can ever underestimate just how great it is to feel valued by your captain or, indeed, your colleagues, and as a team we enjoyed each other's successes. In the next game against South Africa, also in Bridgetown, Swann and I took a combined 5 for 55 in the middle overs to help stifle their reply after we had made 168 for 9. I had Herschelle Gibbs brilliantly caught by Ryan Sidebottom with my first ball, which settled me into my spell straight away, and also bowled Albie Morkel. Sidebottom then picked up three wickets at the end as they were dismissed for 129. We were on a roll.

Picking the same team certainly helped give us confidence and momentum. We only changed the side once when KP had to fly home for the birth of his first child and missed our next game in St Lucia against New Zealand, which we won by three wickets. Swann and Broad both took two wickets while I bowled four tight but wicketless overs for 25 and made a second-ball duck. Tim Bresnan smacked 23 off 11 deliveries at the end to see us into the semi-finals.

Our opponents Sri Lanka had a strong top order and we knew they would be dangerous but by then the squad was infused with so much confidence we honestly fancied ourselves against anyone. KP came back after welcoming his new son into the world and led us to victory with 42 off 26 balls, but our bowling attack had set up the win. We never let their batsmen get going. The seamers, particularly Stuart Broad, bowled aggressively and Swann and I soon settled into our rhythm, conceding 41 runs from our eight overs combined. Angelo Matthews made 58 but their 128 for 6 was well under par, especially once KP got going. With him in the side and playing with so much fluency, we were always confident of chasing a target.

A lot of the credit for the way we bowled in the tournament has to go to bowling coach David Saker, who had just replaced Troy Cooley. He didn't say a lot but when he talked about our plans for each game he demonstrated real clarity of thought. A couple of days before we met Australia in the final he bumped into a few of their backroom staff for a couple of beers and reported back that they were extremely confident they would justify their pre-tournament tag as favourites.

It was just an extra little motivation, not that we needed much. For the first time in the tournament I woke up on the morning of the final feeling nervous but once the game began, in front of stands at the Kensington Oval that seemed to be full of St George and Union Jack flags, I absolutely loved it, even when my bowling got hammered for the first time in the tournament.

We had reduced Australia to 45 for 4 and when Swann and I came on Australia initially found it hard to get us way.

Then, in the 13th over, I conceded 21 runs. David Hussey swiped me for six off the first ball and took a single off the next to bring Cameron White into strike. He hit me for four, six and a four off successive balls and suddenly they had a bit of belief, although if KP hadn't wandered out of position at mid-on when White struck me for his second boundary I would have got him out. He had got under the low full toss I bowled and I turned around expecting to see KP with the ball in his hands. But he'd stationed himself five yards further round because, as he later told me, he thought that was where White was going to hit it! Colly and I exchanged knowing glances and just got on with it but it would have been nice to have taken a wicket in the final.

Instead, Colly took me out of the attack and gave Luke Wright an over, his only one of the tournament. Luke reacted brilliantly under pressure considering he probably didn't expect to be bowling. He got his yorker going straight away and eventually frustrated White who had a wild swipe outside off stump and Stuart Broad ran back to take the catch just in front of the cover boundary. That was a massive moment for us.

The Hussey brothers, David and Michael, added 47 in four overs for the sixth wicket but we felt their total of 147 for 6 was at least 20 runs short. Our batsmen approached the run chase with the same attacking intent they had shown throughout the tournament. There was certainly no need for Colly to say anything at the mid-innings break and the rest of us settled back in the dugout to enjoy the fun as Craig

Kieswetter and KP took on their attack after the early loss of Michael Lumb to Shaun Tait.

After the power play we were 41 for 1, compared to Australia's 24 for 3, and had built our platform. We then took 16 off an over from Shane Watson and even when KP holed out for 47 we only needed 30 off seven overs. Kieswetter's magnificent innings ended on 63 from 49 balls and Colly and Eoin Morgan were left to see us to victory. The pre-match plan was that if Morgan had got out Luke Wright or Tim Bresnan would have gone in next. If it had been the captain, I would have replaced him. But then, while they were knocking off the runs, Andy Flower told me to be ready to bat whoever got out. There I was, enjoying the show and all of a sudden it dawned on me that I might have to see us home. I was as nervous as hell. Every run they got nearer the target was cheered as loudly by me in the dugout as any England supporter in the sun-drenched stands. It was only when Colly hit a six and four off Watson to bring the scores level that I could finally relax. A few moments later we were rushing onto the outfield to mob the skipper. We were World Cup winners. Champions.

For the second game in a row I was picked out for the drugs test so while the rest of the squad prepared for their lap of honour I was desperately trying to pee into a plastic bottle. It was a bit surreal walking around the ground in front of thousands of England supporters, a lot of whom had flown in for the game, for our lap of honour while the Australia and New Zealand women's teams were trying to prepare for their final. In all the mayhem the organisers forgot to bring the boundary rope in for them which might explain why only six boundaries were scored in their match! Fair play to the Australian men, who all stayed to watch their women achieve what they couldn't do.

The groundstaff were trying to lock up when we finally left the dressing rooms late in the afternoon. The 9.30am start to the final at least meant we could enjoy a day-long celebration, which continued back at the team hotel where the ECB had laid on a reception and carried on in the bars of Bridgetown long into the night. We were an unlikely team of winners. When the squad was announced the press picked holes in it and I don't think too many people gave us much of a chance in the tournament itself, never mind the final. But we had that all-important commodity after the scare against Ireland – momentum. The team was settled, we all knew our roles and we all enjoyed each other's successes.

Personally, it was a great moment. When you are captain, as I was of Sussex by then, you live the wins and losses a lot more, you take it to heart a bit. But I went into the World Cup on the back of a great season at home and was bowling as well as at any stage of my career in one-day cricket. For a lot of our opponents I was probably seen as our weak link so I'm proud that I had changed one or two opinions by the end of the tournament. Back home, Karin watched it with some friends on TV. I guess my only tiny regret is that she wasn't there to enjoy the moment with me.

It was great to enjoy the celebrations with a Sussex team-mate as well in Luke Wright. Luke went on to play 100 games for England yet now, at the age of 30 and looking forward to leading the county for the first time in 2016, I think he's a better cricketer than he was during the time when he played most of his cricket for England. He's still got massive power, a fantastic eye and by playing in T20 tournaments around the globe, against some of the world's best bowlers, he has gained even more valuable experience. I would have taken him to this year's World Cup in India. He's an exceptional talent who still has so much to offer, a real global star of the T20 age.

One-day cricket has moved on so much in the intervening six years and England's fortunes have rocketed up the graph since the last 50-over World Cup in 2015. So why did it take us so long to adopt the fearless, attack-at-all-costs approach which has been the hallmark of Eoin Morgan's teams in the last 12 months or so? Why didn't we play like that before when so many other countries were? I certainly think we had the personnel, but we've always been held back by that deep-rooted English sense of conservatism, despite the best intentions of a succession of coaches and captains going back two decades or even longer. We seem to have this fear that we start to try to score at seven or eight runs an over we will run the risk, more often than not, of being bowled out for 80. Far better, it seemed for years, to try and scrape together 220 to stay in the game but then watch helplessly as the opposition rattle to their target with 15 or 20 overs to spare. Eoin Morgan must take a lot of the credit. He came in last year and basically said, 'I don't care if we get rolled over for spit now and again. We have the batting talent and we shouldn't be wasting it.'

I'd have loved to have been part of the squad that scored 400 against New Zealand in 2015, it was so refreshing to see.

I'd like to see a T20 franchise league, similar to the ones they have in Australia and the Caribbean, in this country as well. Sorry, I really don't know how you could do it and keep all 18 first-class counties onside but the more our players are exposed to the best bowlers in the world the better, especially when we go to places like India and the subcontinent where we have traditionally struggled in the past.

With the benefit of hindsight, it would have been perfect if my England career had ended that sunny May Sunday in Barbados. Instead, it was the start of my most consistent period in the team. Between June 2010 and my exit from the 2011 World Cup I played in a further 22 one-day internationals and four T20s. In fact, just six weeks after the final I was in the team that played Scotland in a one-day international in Edinburgh.

But I knew I had serious problems, the happy hours which followed the World Cup triumph having long since been consigned to the memory. And despite the feelings of anxiety and helplessness which were starting to envelop me I did have some good days during the summer of 2010 and the early winter of 2011 in Australia. I became a bit more consistent with the bat having finally found a settled role thanks to Andy Flower, initially at No.6 and then in 2011 at No. 7 in the longer format. I scored two half-centuries, both against Australia, and although there were days when I was a bit expensive with the ball there weren't too many. But I was enjoying the experience less and less. As I explained in the early chapters of this book, a few months after winning the World Cup – which was one of the most unforgettable experiences of my life – playing for England became something I didn't want to do.

The ill-fated and thankfully one-off experiment of me batting at No.3 came at Lord's against Australia in July 2010 and it was the only time in my career when I thought the bowling was too quick for me to handle. KP had hurt his hamstring and had pulled out of the team. Andy Flower was meticulous in his preparations but I don't remember him applying a very scientific method to choosing me as his replacement as he walked around the dressing room eyeing up potential candidates before pointing at me! Shaun Tait had already ripped the ball past Andrew Strauss's defensive prod to claim his first wicket with the speed gun registering 98mph when I walked into the coconut shy. I had to wander past Tait on my way to the wicket and he was waiting for me. "Where's the big show, Yards?" referring to KP. I told him he'd done his hamstring and prepared to face the music.

His first delivery whistled past my off stump and I literally didn't see it. That's when I thought he was too quick for me. The next ball cut me in half as it jagged back off the seam and flew to the boundary for four byes after the wicketkeeper Tim Paine missed it as well. I had to smile when Paine and the slips started giving me the verbals. After all, Paine was a further 30 yards back and he'd still waved it all the way to the boundary rope! The next ball was a fraction wide and, as I went to leave it, it nipped back and cannoned into my off stump. Gone for a duck. Outclassed really. As I trudged back, Ricky Ponting, the Australia captain, sided up to me. "Hey Yards, you're never a No.3. Get yourself back down to six or seven." He might have even had a bit of sympathy for me. As I neared the pavilion steps the Sky cameraman who was alongside me piped up. "If it's any consolation they have registered that delivery at 100mph." I know speed cameras have always been notoriously untrustworthy but those were certainly the quickest three balls I ever faced in my career. It was not a pleasant experience.

So there you have the answer to the question 'who was the quickest bowler you've ever faced?' The best batsman might surprise you a bit. The one player who I couldn't believe hit the ball as hard as he did was Australia's Damien Martyn. I remember fielding at mid-on when he was batting against us during the Champions Trophy in 2007 in Jaipur and he played a checked drive off Steve Harmison that nearly took my hand off. It probably would have done if he'd really got hold of the shot. He wasn't a power hitter but the strength he generated from his wrists was unbelievable. No one I faced before or since for England hit the ball with such brutal power and timing. His wrists must have had steel ball bearings in them!

When I started to work on this book I was asked what I'd do differently if I had my time with England all over again. I think I embraced being an England player on the pitch but, as I've explained, I didn't always enjoy what came with the job away from the games themselves. By 2011 I was going downhill fast mentally. Playing for England had become such a massive strain. Yet a few weeks earlier, during the one-day series in Australia and, of course, during the 2010 T20 World Cup, I really tried hard to enjoy the off-field stuff. When the bad times came, and with no support network close at hand to fall back on in terms of Karin, life with England became a constant struggle. I know Brett Morrissey or the other counsellors I worked with at the time were only a phone call away but I have to admit that often it was easier not to have to contact people, even if they could help me. Sometimes I thought, 'I don't want to discuss all this crap anymore. I just want it to go away.' That was the illness talking, not me. And it was taking over.

Of course I've still got my 2010 World Cup winners' medal. It is on display in the Sussex Library at Hove but I'm in no rush to get it back. The ECB framed and individually numbered from 1 to 100 a picture of the victorious squad and that is hanging in my lounge at our home in Brighton, but it's the only memento I have on display in the house. There are a few shirts, from when I made my debut and other important games, in the loft but I auctioned a lot of memorabilia during my benefit and I'm neither a great hoarder nor someone who wants to have their career on display. Put it this way, you'll never see me building an extension to show off all my cricket bits and pieces!

What I do have though are memories, and not just of successful days with England such as Barbados in 2010. Often you remember the sacrifices you made to be able to pull on an England shirt – those early morning runs in the middle of winter when it's raining hard and freezing cold so you were in the best possible shape when you arrived for events like the T20 World Cup. They will always mean more to me than shirts and medals.

8

Sussex by the Sea

THE Sussex players who were involved in the most successful decade in the history of the county will be old and grey – or in some cases greyer – when it finally sinks in just what we all achieved during those magical few years between 2003–09. I know I will be.

We had some very talented individuals of course and not even the most blinkered of Sussex supporters could seriously suggest that we would have won so many trophies during that period without the stellar contributions of Mushtaq Ahmed and Murray Goodwin. But there was a lot more to Sussex than that. I believe that the team ethic fostered initially by Peter Moores, which Mark Robinson built upon when he became coach at the end of 2005 was absolutely crucial to what we achieved. Without the togetherness and sense of unity that we had we wouldn't have won anything, never mind the eight trophies that Grizzly did lift in his 11 seasons as our skipper.

The buzzwords at the time were 'The Sussex Way'. But what exactly was that? I got asked the question a few times by our opponents, normally after we'd beaten them. We appreciated what each of us brought to the overall effort and we enjoyed each other's successes – as well as our own of course. And for those years when we were the best team in the country we were fitter than anyone else, better prepared and always ready to play hard at a time when the standard of domestic cricket was as high as it had been for years. Teams were queueing up to take down these upstarts from the south coast, whom they perceived as a one-man (Mushy) or, if they were feeling generous, two-man (Mushy and Murray) team. After all, before 2003 Sussex had only won a handful of one-day trophies and their last major success had been the NatWest victory at Lord's in 1986, way before any of our times.

The one game from that era which sticks out for me was our Championship match against Lancashire at Liverpool in August 2007. We'd been badly beaten inside two days up there 14 months earlier and when we reconvened at Aigburth both sides were vying to win the title. There were 13 international cricketers taking part – including five from Sussex – and as soon as we arrived and saw that the pitch would provide good carry and bounce for the bowlers and the small boundaries would give batsmen full value for their shots we knew that there would be a positive result and that whoever won would have the initiative going into the last few weeks of the season.

If it had been up to me I wouldn't have been playing, as I will explain later, but I'm glad I did. I never played Test cricket but this was probably what it was like, and I know I'm not the only one of the nine non-Test cricketers who took part that felt exactly the same. There was a lot of needle and a few of us had personal agendas, not least Lancashire's talisman Andrew Flintoff who bowled for the first time since an ankle operation two months earlier and was desperate to prove his fitness to the England selectors.

In the first innings I went for my shots and scored 47, a decent contribution for me because I was so badly out of form at the time. After tea on the second day we went in to bat again 27 runs behind and straight away lost Chris Nash and Richard Montgomerie, our openers, with just two runs on the board. But Murray Goodwin and I negotiated the final session without further loss against an attack that also included Glen Chapple, Muttiah Muralitharan and Dominic Cork as well as a fired-up Flintoff on the third morning. At the close I'd got to 52 not out and was desperate to cash in the next day. I was convinced I was going to score a century. Unfortunately, in the first over next morning, I got a very thin tickle down the leg side off Cork and was out. It was my first Championship half-century of the season but I should have gone on. No matter, we set them 242 to win but when they reached 65 for 1 just after tea it looked as if we might struggle to take the game into a fourth day, when rain was forecast.

But then Robin Martin-Jenkins, who had a wonderful knack of getting us a wicket or two when we needed it, picked up Mal Loye and Brad Hodge in quick succession and they started wobbling. Grizz then pulled off a fantastic catch at slip to remove our old nemesis Stuart Law, who always seemed to get big runs against us. That was the turning point. Mushtaq Ahmed, who'd come into the attack in the fifth over, and Rana Naved mopped up the rest with a combination of googlies and unplayable reverse swing and we ended up winning by 108 runs. That was what it said in the paper the next day anyway. In truth it felt like we'd squeezed home by ten runs or something. A bit like what we used to do to teams, Lancashire had kept coming at us.

I think that game epitomised what we were about as a team more than any other during this golden period for Sussex. We didn't give Lancashire an inch on a ground where they had a tremendous record and we fought hard for every run against a world-class attack. We didn't play great cricket all of the time, particularly during 2007, but we knew how to win dirty if we had to, and by that I don't mean with underhand tactics. With Mushy in the side our game plan was simple and we always knew if we could get 350 or 400 on the board, especially batting first, we were in control with a player like him up our sleeve.

Grizz was still as committed and combative a captain as ever that year, despite nearly leaving in October 2006 to join Yorkshire. I have to admit I found the whole scenario quite difficult to deal with at the time. The first I knew something was up was when I read about it in the *Brighton Argus;* there had been no warning for the players from the management that something big was about to break. Chris's father John is from Huddersfield, Chris was born only a few miles from the Yorkshire border in north Derbyshire and when he said that he'd always wanted to play for the White Rose I could understand that. The job itself – which was basically to oversee the first team and their professional cricket operation as well as captain the team – looked too good to turn down, a fantastic opportunity.

What didn't sit well with me at the time was when Grizz realised the job wasn't all it was cracked up to be, having even been introduced to the media and held up a Yorkshire shirt for the cameras. He came back to Sussex and expected to be welcomed back with open arms. I guess at the time I had the mentality of a football fan who sees their favourite player, who had spent years at the club and enjoyed wonderful success, suddenly swapping allegiances, wearing the shirt of another team, kissing the badge and saying joining the club was something he always wanted to do. Between going to Yorkshire and then deciding to stay at Sussex, Mark Robinson and the chairman, David Green, sounded out a few of us – Murray Goodwin, James Kirtley, Matt Prior and Richard Montgomerie as well as myself – about taking over as captain and now we were asked to carry on as if nothing had happened.

At the start of 2007 I had a frank conversation with Grizz, expressing my misgivings about what had happened, but we moved on and after that I was fine. There was certainly no problem with our relationship. Indeed, by the time the squad came together in March for pre-season training it was as if nothing had happened, although to be honest that's the same scenario when any player leaves a club. I don't imagine at the start of 2016 that the Sussex lads gave a second thought to the fact that I wasn't with them anymore. You move on quickly. Every season is like a fresh start even if the personnel has not changed that much.

Grizz stayed on as captain after leading us to our third Championship in 2007. I think he felt that Mushtaq had one more good season left in him and that he could help us to win more trophies but there were signs of things to come during 2007, which was by far the hardest of the three we enjoyed in five seasons to win. We really had to grind it out. I was still recovering from my broken finger when we lost back to back games to Warwickshire and Kent by an innings at the start of the season. The defeat at Canterbury was followed by a heart-to-heart among the management and players and a determination to get back to basics. We won the next game against Worcestershire at New Road by an innings and went on an undefeated run that lasted for the next 11 matches.

But as a squad, we just didn't have the depth that year to challenge across all three formats as we had done in 2006. With Mushy still in the team the emphasis was still on four-day cricket, particularly in the first half of the season when we needed to get back on track after those two early setbacks. As a result, our defence of the Friends Provident Trophy never got going. There was a lot of rain around, but we only won one game in the group stages.

I had started so well of course with 99 against the MCC at Lord's but when Steve Harmison shattered my finger it not only sidelined me for nearly two months but it then took me just as long to rediscover any semblance of form and by the time we went to Liverpool for that huge game against Lancashire I was ready to step out of the team.

It was the first time since I started using exaggerated trigger movements at the crease in 2004 that I felt they weren't working. I lost so much rhythm when I was not playing and when I came back I was so desperate to do well that I quickly settled into a tiring routine of practice, play, practice. I over-did it, when what I needed to do really was relax and work things through in the practice nets. Instead I felt so tense and wasn't a good presence in the dressing room at all. Could those few weeks have triggered the problems I experienced during the England Lions' tour to India the following winter? Perhaps.

I thought I'd found some belated form in mid-July when I scored a century against Sri Lanka A at Hove but in our next Championship game against Hampshire at the Rose Bowl I scored a single in both innings and felt like I was back to square one again. It was an awful four days. We batted first in gloomy light and the team were upset when the umpires called for the floodlights to be switched on without asking his permission. It was a real struggle to pick up the red ball in that odd mix of artificial and floodlight and, on a damp pitch prepared to negate Mushy and which did a lot for the seam bowlers, we were soon struggling on 64 for 6. There was no play at all on the second day and because of the fractious relationship between Grizz and his rival captain Shane Warne, who were barely on speaking terms at the time, there was never much chance of a deal being done to set up a run chase for the last day.

Instead, I remember going out to bat, briefly as it turned out, in the second innings and being on the end of constant abuse from Warne, standing in the slips like he owned the place. Which, in truth, he probably did. He seemed to have made up his mind that my brief return to the England team for the one-day series against West Indies a few weeks earlier would be my international swansong and he let me know in no uncertain terms. Warne knew how to rub someone up the wrong way – in fact he was a master at it. I remember he was just as vocal about my abilities, or lack of them as he saw it, a couple of years earlier but that day I scored a century against Hampshire and because I was playing so well none of his bullshit got through. When you're out of nick you hear every word. But playing against him was fantastic and I could only admire the way he bought into county cricket with so much passion and, of course, the skill he still had as a brilliant bowler.

I had no answers. When I found myself out of form later in my career I used to respond by having a dip, going for my shots and trying to put pressure on the opposition bowlers but back then the only solution seemed to tough it out. As we were packing up after the game I told Mark Robinson that if he wanted to change the batting and drop me so I could get some form back in the seconds I would be fine about it but Robbo was having none of it. He said at the start of the season, when I was injured, that my absence at No.3 had been very evident. He believed that when I was playing well it reassured the rest of the team and gave the dressing room an air of calmness. But I wasn't playing well so how was I helping the team now? He told me that I was too good a player to be out of nick for long. He trusted me to get it back. In truth, I also suspect Robbo knew there weren't too many players not in the side pressing for inclusion through weight of runs in the second team. He was always a fiercely loyal coach during his time at Sussex.

In the game after we beat Lancashire I made 54 in the second innings as we drew with Warwickshire, thanks mainly to a magnificent 195 from Richard Montgomerie who batted for a day and a half to save us from defeat. Monty, like the rest of us, suffered from dips in form but he was different to me in that he had masses of self-belief. He always thought, after he'd spent a bit of time in the nets, that he could get it back, that his natural ability would pull him through a bad spell. Monty was a great team-mate because he had no agenda whatsoever. Whatever he did was for the team, whether it was playing innings like that one against Warwickshire, which was absolutely crucial in terms of our chances of retaining the title, showing brilliant anticipation to snaffle catches under the helmet at boot hill, usually off Mushy of course, or coming up with the answer to a fiendishly difficult clue in *The Times'* cryptic crossword that the rest of us had been struggling with in the dressing room for hours. He maybe wasn't a natural leader, but he's the sort of person every team needed in order to be successful. It was a sad day for Sussex when he announced his retirement at the end of the 2007 season so he could start a career in teaching.

So after that Warwickshire match we were still in there fighting for the title but we then spent four frustrating days at The Oval watching the rain fall. The match was abandoned without a ball bowled, the first time that had happened there since 1981. Some of our rivals were faltering too but when we went into our penultimate home game against the leaders Yorkshire, ourselves, Lancashire and Durham also had a realistic chance of being the champions. It was hugely frustrating not to play the Surrey game but in hindsight the break might have done us good because we returned against Yorkshire and thrashed them.

We beat Yorkshire by an innings and 261 runs at Hove, which we were staggered to read afterwards was their biggest defeat since 1898. They had nine internationals in their team including Inzamam-ul-Haq, who has joined them for a brief spell, but we were all over them from ball one. I made my most significant contribution of the season with 119 while Andy Hodd, who had come into the team for Matt Prior, scored his first Championship hundred. The three Pakistanis in our team – Mushtaq, Saqlain Mushtaq and Rana Naved – were desperate to do well against their former captain. Mushy got Inzy out in the first innings and I don't remember him enjoying a wicket as much during his career, with the possible exception of when he got Brad Hodge out to claim his 100th of the season against Leicestershire in the title-winning game in 2003. Between them, our three Pakistanis took 13 of the wickets to fall and Rana (46) and Saqlain (57) also contributed with the bat against a demoralised attack.

Rana's contribution to our successful era is sometimes overlooked but it's certainly not been forgotten by those who played with him. I loved the guy to bits. He was such a skilful bowler and, when he was in the mood, a wonderfully uninhibited batsman too. He was also a bit of an oddball, right from the time he joined us in 2005 and took to bowling with a sweatband on his head, aka Dennis Lillee from back in the 1970s. Every time he took a wicket he'd run off shouting his name at the top of his voice and every time he encountered our coach at the time he'd shout out "Peter Moores! Peter Moores!" Once, when Pete was about to give us a bollocking at lunch after a poor session, he walked in greeting him like that and even Pete fell about in hysterics.

I lost count of the number of times he'd come back after getting caught on the boundary moaning "I didn't see him! I didn't see that third man!" and then, of course, when he returned to the club for a second spell he'd undergone a hair transplant and suddenly had this mass of thick black curls, which he grew out at the back for added effect, where there had once been a bald bonce. With the bat Rana could be hit or miss but he was so proud to score a hundred at Lord's during our record-breaking partnership in 2005. He'd be swinging from the hip and then strolling nonchalantly down the pitch after I'd played and missed telling me to concentrate! When he pinned his ears back Rana was as quick as anything on the circuit at the time and he was happy to pass on his knowledge of reverse swing to our other bowlers, who all benefitted as a result, in particular Jason Lewry.

Jason was also clever and talented enough to put what he learned into practice. In some ways, Jason was a bit like Mushy. On certain days he could give off the impression that bowling was a huge effort – the pitch was flat, the ball wasn't swinging – but underneath he had massive self-belief, it was just that he kept it very well hidden. Of all the bowlers I played with Jason was up there among the very best, he had so much natural talent. Of course he should have played for England but I don't think that ever motivated him. He'd come into the county game relatively late from club cricket at the age of 23 and just enjoyed doing the day job, simple as that.

He had no ego whatsoever and when he got a good player out, which he used to do for fun it seemed, he could never understand what all the fuss was about. "Well, that's what I'm here to do isn't it?" would invariably be his response. I remember one of my first games for Sussex against Hampshire in 2001 when a sea fret rolled in at Hove and he took 13 wickets in the match and seven in 14 balls at one stage in their second innings. I recall Adrian Aymes, the Hampshire wicketkeeper, taking guard about two feet outside leg stump to try and negate the swing and still falling lbw as he shuffled in front of a massive inducker.

Sometimes, though, he would need a little prod to produce his best. We played India in 2007 when I was captain, having belatedly taken over after being released from the England one-day squad, and their very strong batting line-up – VVS Laxman, Gautam Gambhir, Rahul Dravid and MS Dhoni – were all enjoying an extended net on a flat pitch. In the second innings I wound Jason up a treat. "Look, Jase, if you could keep it down to seven runs an over that would be good." He stared at me, nodded and then next ball produced this brilliant outswinger which Dhoni nibbled at and was caught in the slips. Matt Prior also knew that the occasional wind-up would get the best out of Jason, on the slow Hove pitches at that time in particular. "Come on Jase, see if you can get it to carry to me," was his oft-used line. It was normally enough to wake the beast.

If Matt had tried that on James Kirtley he would probably have been throttled. From the days when he used to pick me up at Eastbourne Station I never came across a more driven, intense and focussed cricketer – team-mate or opponent – than James. I think it used to annoy the hell out of him when he would be busting a gut on our dead Hove wickets trying to make things happen and Jason would just amble in off four or five paces and get a wicket more or less straight away. James had the strength of character to rebuild his career and reputation not once but twice when he was reported for an illegal bowling action and we were all thrilled for him when he got one last England hurrah at the end of the 2007 season in the inaugural T20 World Cup in South Africa.

It was no more than he deserved after spearheading our own run to the domestic finals day that year with 13 wickets and an economy rate of 7.42 runs per over – which was very respectable. My own involvement in the group stages was limited because of England commitments but we thrashed Yorkshire in the quarter-final at Hove and were made favourites to win the tournament. That didn't sit comfortably with me, not then and subsequently again when I was captain. You could see why we were so well fancied though. Matt Prior was back from England duties for the semi-final against Kent and we had two world-class spinners in Mushy and Saqlain, ideal for the dry, slow Edgbaston wicket. And we headed straight to Edgbaston for the finals on the back of that brilliant Championship victory against Lancashire at Liverpool.

And it all started so well. We were 60 without loss after 5.1 overs but ended up getting bowled out for 140, which was probably 10–15 runs short. My own contribution was 4 runs and running out Grizz, when he was going well on 15. I felt mortified at the time but there was redemption of sorts a year or so later when the squad sat down to watch some footage our analyst had put together on the best techniques of diving in to the crease to make your ground. During the bit on how not to do it, they showed Grizz diving in legs first during the Kent semi-final. It looked terrible – and it clearly wasn't my fault. When Kent batted we ran them close but Rob Key made a classy, unbeaten 68 and Rana bowled a couple of no-balls in the last over and they won with four deliveries to spare and went on to defeat Gloucestershire, who had surprised Lancashire in the other semi, in the final.

It's a shame we didn't see the best of Saqlain during his time at Sussex because of his knee problems but he was excellent for us when he did play, particularly in one-day cricket, and so was another Pakistani, Yasir Arafat. He was a great player to captain and on the days when he slipped himself he could bowl very quickly. He had a great yorker, which on some occasions it seemed he could bowl to order, and was another player who made a big contribution to our success in one-day cricket. It helped, of course, that they all respected Mushy so much, who was something of a father figure to them and instrumental in the signing of both Saqlain and Yasir. If any of them ever had a problem, they would go and see Mushy and he'd take it up with Robbo on their behalf. If he thought they weren't at their best Mushy would have a quiet word or invite them round, with the rest of us, to his house where either he or Yasir would cook – curry, of course – and deliver a little pep talk. And if Mushy had a problem – like his TV had packed up – he'd come to me and ask me to sort it out.

Mind you, not even Mushy's best curry could have eased the pain Rana felt when he dislocated his shoulder in our penultimate Championship game of 2007 at the Riverside against Durham. After trying to make a typically wholehearted stop on the boundary, he was in such agony that the game was halted for 45 minutes before an ambulance drove over the outfield and took him off to hospital. A few hours later he was back with us on the team coach as we headed down the A1 having lost by nine wickets. Every time the bus went over a bump in the road Rana would squeal in agony, even though he was dosed up with painkillers. With Saqlain hobbling on one leg and Murray Goodwin due to return to Australia as soon as we got back to Hove because of a family bereavement we were struggling to field anything like our best side for the final fixture against Worcestershire, which we had to win and hope other results went our way if we were to win a third title.

Lancashire started the final round of games six points clear and I was convinced they would beat Surrey, who had nothing to play for, at The Oval in their final fixture. At the start of the final day of the season Durham, who had defeated Kent in three days, were actually leading the table but we duly did our bit as Mushtaq produced probably his last great performance for us, taking 13 Worcestershire wickets on a slow deck to enable us to beat them by an innings. We wrapped up victory before lunch; all we could do now was wait for the Surrey–Lancashire match to be decided.

Far from throwing in the towel, Surrey dominated the game and set Lancashire 489 to win from 106 overs. To get to within 25 runs of winning was a fantastic effort by Lancashire but shortly after 6pm, with hundreds of Sussex supporters sitting on the outfield following the game in a myriad of different ways, there was a huge roar and the title was ours. We'd been unable to access Sky Sports' live coverage from The Oval on the TV in our dressing room so it became a very long afternoon during which I got slowly pissed. At one point Matt Prior had the bright idea of going to his house a few hundred yards from the ground to get his Sky remote control to see if that might enable us to access the pictures from The Oval. I went with him but instead of heading straight back to the ground we ended up sitting on his sofa for more than an hour, knocking back a bottle of champagne between us and catching up. I don't even think we watched the cricket – we were more interested in the football scores instead. When we eventually returned to the dressing room I fell asleep and was just about awake when the news came through that we were champions again, though quite how I managed to stand up straight for the subsequent trophy presentation given how much alcohol I'd consumed is still something I can't work out.

Our third Championship in four years then but, even with Grizzly still at the helm and Mushy due back for another year, I sensed it might be our last for a while. We had limped over the line and the team was not as settled as it had been in 2003 and 2006, with only four of the players – Adams, Montgomerie, Chris Nash and Mushtaq – playing in all of our 15 completed games. By the end Mushy, in particular, was really struggling with his knees. It was always our hope that after a winter off he would return in 2008 rejuvenated but he was not much fitter at the start of the year despite having some surgery during the winter and finally succumbed halfway through that season. He announced his retirement with immediate effect, having taken 476 Championship wickets and been the country's leading wicket-taker for five seasons in a row from 2003. By then, what was keeping him on the field was purely his strength of mind. Even at the end, when he was hobbling off to his fielding position between overs, he still thought he could do anything on the cricket field.

Of course I'd have loved to have had the chance to captain Mushy on a regular basis but I didn't envy Grizz in one way – his occasional inability to actually get the ball out of Mushy's hands. With Mushy, even if he'd been toiling away for 20 overs or more without reward, it was always his belief that a wicket wasn't far away. I always admired Mushy, he always had time for everyone and it did not matter what their stature in life or in the game was. He also had a mischievous side and loved to wind people up. He would love to challenge his team-mates to a sporting event. I remember once at Canterbury, when we were playing Kent, he challenged Tony Cottey, who was the fittest player on the staff at the time, to a race of two laps of the outfield. Mushy sent off at an impressive pace but by the start of the second lap Cotts had just gone past him. Mushy stopped and it was not until Cotts was around the other side of the field that he realised it was no longer a two-horse race. For the rest of the game Mushy was adamant that it was a one-lap race and he had won. I suppose the competitiveness and total self belief were traits that helped make him him the exceptional player he was.

Mushy knew people everywhere – Manchester, Leeds, London, Birmingham – and invariably there would be an open invitation to visit one of the best Indian restaurants in the city where he was treated like a VIP and we tucked in, always on the house of course.

A night in a curry house, even socialising with my team-mates, was the last thing on my mind in the first half of 2008.

I have always been introverted, but after all the problems I suffered in India earlier that winter I quickly fell into a routine that I felt I could just about manage: train, play, spend time with the family. I think I hid my fragile state of mind very well, certainly for those first few weeks of the 2008 season, but my form as we made a stuttering defence of our title – one win in the first eight games – was pretty poor. Everything had become a chore, being at home was the only time I felt in any way relaxed and happy.

Things came to a head when we lost to Lancashire at Hove at the beginning of July – and not just for me. I made 25 and 36, which in the context of our overall performance was not too bad – but I felt terrible. We lost by eight wickets and suffered our second successive defeat at Hove, having gone four years without losing there prior to losing to Durham a couple of weeks earlier. Mushy got through 33 overs but I'm not sure how. He was virtually on one knee but the old fizz wasn't there. A couple of days later he was back under the knife but he didn't play for Sussex again.

It was the end of an era and another was coming to a close as well. Mark Robinson gave me some time off after the Lancashire game which helped tremendously and not long after I came back both he and Jim May, who had taken over from David Green as chairman, started talking to me about becoming captain. Grizzly was going to step down at the end of the season after 11 years in charge.

The timing was perfect for me. If I'd been approached by the club in the first two months of the season I would have run a mile from the job. But after being sounded out the more I thought about the job the more energised I became by the thought of leading the team. Karin gave birth to Raffy, our second-born, in August and that improved my mood as well. She was also fully supportive of my decision to accept the captaincy if it was officially offered to me. One or two of my friends, mainly club sponsors who I saw socially now and again, had their doubts and told me so but I didn't really care what they felt to be honest. I don't mean that in a selfish way, it's just that there were only a handful of people whose opinions I really valued at that time. It was a very small circle at Sussex during this time– Mark Robinson, Peter Moores, Keith Greenfield, James Kirtley, Matt Prior and Carl Hopkinson. If you're in that circle, you're in. For me to really trust someone they have to be very close to me. I don't let people in easily, I never have done.

My Championship form picked up in the second half of the 2008 season, but for the first time since 2004 I didn't score a first-class hundred, finishing with 899 runs at an average of 37.45. We beat Hampshire at Arundel to claim our second win of the campaign and it was enough to make sure we avoided the fate of Nottinghamshire and Yorkshire who had been relegated immediately after winning the title. Without Mushy, as we all had feared, winning four-day games was suddenly a lot more difficult. Our performances in the T20 were pretty abysmal, with just two wins from our ten games.

But some good results in the Pro40 kept the season alive and it was during our final home game, when we beat Middlesex at Hove, that the changing of the guard took place. The rest of the lads were told at Trent Bridge the day before our final Pro40 game against Nottinghamshire which we needed to win to send Grizz off into retirement with another trophy. As he spoke, Grizz was clearly very upset. His reaction surprised me, but it shouldn't have done. Being captain of Sussex had been a massive part of his life and to give it up was extremely hard for him. He was desperate to stay at the club in some sort of capacity, but although he was interviewed for the job of chief executive it went to Dave Brooks instead, who proved to be an excellent appointment and was very supportive to me as captain. A few weeks after the season ended he followed Brooks' predecessor Gus Mackay to Surrey and his first coaching role.

Thanks to Murray Goodwin the Adams era ended in style although it didn't look that way when we slumped from 87 for 2, after I was out to Samit Patel for 53, to 130 for 8 in the 30th over. Murray was still in but with only Mohammad Sami, our overseas locum, and James Kirtley left to bat, our target of 227 looked beyond us.

But Murray was in the mood that day. Sami gave him good support, even though his limited English made even the most basic instructions difficult. I think Murray eventually just told him if it was there to be hit to hit it! Anyway, they whittled away at the target and with a boundary needed off the last ball to win he rocked back deep into his crease and swung Charlie Shreck over the rope for six. Only Murray could have played that sort of innings. He had a ruthlessness once he got going which would be evident whether he was playing in front of a full house at Lord's or half a dozen spectators and a dog on a damp morning in Derby. He was the best player I batted with by a mile, although I think Matt Prior would have had a similar record to his for Sussex had his England career not taken off in the way it did. Murray was always willing to help others with their game, but he could get exasperated when us mere mortals got out playing daft shots. But like everyone who played for Sussex during that era it was all about the team. Individual accolades always came second.

Moments after Murray won the game for us, Grizz was being presented with the trophy and tearfully confirming that it was his last game as a Sussex player, never mind captain.

The Michael Yardy era was underway.

9

Captain

I N the winter of 2008/09, when I wasn't constantly making sure the house in Perth wasn't about to be burgled, I spent a lot of time thinking about what sort of captain I wanted to be.

It's not as if I had played under a lot of them and could pick out the best or worst of their traits. At Sussex it had been Chris Adams and more or less no one else since I joined the club and with England I'd just about got used to playing under someone when the tour or series was over. In any case, there's only so much you take in as a player from your captain, especially at international level. Most of the time all you are worrying about is yourself and your own form.

I had regular chats on the phone from Australia with Sussex coach Mark Robinson discussing who we might bring in to replace the irreplaceable in Mushtaq Ahmed as overseas player and how our own captain–coach relationship would develop. The most important thing we did agree on was that we were going to make a massive push to improve our one-day performances. We'd won a couple of trophies but for many of the previous few years limited-overs success tended to be regarded as a nice but unexpected bonus at Sussex, even though we were usually regarded as a team to watch in the white-ball formats because we had been successful in four-day cricket.

With Mushy in the team we were geared up to try to win the Championship and I had no problem with that at all, but we needed to rethink our strategy and try to be successful without him.

As well as a new captain there was a freshness to the squad as some younger players started to really come through and that definitely helped me ease into the role. Grizzly and Richard Montgomerie had gone and by the end of 2010 two more stalwarts of Sussex's Championship-winning era – James Kirtley and Robin Martin-Jenkins – had retired, Jason Lewry having packed up a year earlier. Like me, they had only really known one Sussex captain whereas some of the younger lads had played very little cricket under Chris Adams so they did not really have anyone to compare me to.

In terms of personnel, the priority that winter was to find an experienced batsman and we were fortunate to land Ed Joyce. I knew Ed from touring with England Lions together and we'd had a tentative chat about his future plans in India in 2007. We spoke again the following summer but when Ed led

Middlesex to an unexpected T20 title in 2008 I didn't think we had any chance of signing him.

But I heard on the grapevine towards the end of the season, just after I found out I would be taking over as captain, that he was still looking to leave Middlesex and that Nottinghamshire, who would probably have been able to offer him a better contract, were keen on signing him as well. That's why it was so important, or at least I felt it was at the time, that we retained our first division status in the Championship. I didn't think Ed, who still had ambitions to play Test cricket for England, would want to play in the second division but, to my surprise, he later told me that was not a factor in his decision to join us.

A few weeks after the season finished I drove up to Loughborough for an England Lions training camp. Ed was there too but on the way up the M1 his car broke down outside Luton and he was left stranded by the side of the motorway. He rang to see if I'd set off, hoping that I hadn't done so he could be picked up on the way north. I had come up the previous evening though, but as I had nothing much to do I hopped in my car and drove back down the M1 to collect him.

I didn't think anything more of it at the time. All I'd done was pick up a friend who needed some help but Ed felt my gesture epitomised what Sussex was all about. Mates who looked out for each other on and off the pitch and who always put the team first. It was something I was keen would continue under my captaincy and just before I headed off to

Australia we signed Ed on a three-year contract which was fantastic news.

Although I was looking forward to being in charge, if Ed had insisted that a prerequisite of him coming to Sussex was to captain the side as well I would happily have stepped aside and been his deputy. One concession I did make was to let Ed bat at No.3 which meant I would have to revert back to opening the batting, which I'd started to do again since 2008, on a permanent basis. It was hardly ideal for a captain to be opening as well and I loved batting at three, but I was happy to move to accommodate a talented player like Ed. And when we did speak after he signed he insisted on telling me he had no designs on the captaincy back then. He wanted a fresh start and to win trophies for himself. He'd come to the right place as it turned out.

2009 was my most enjoyable season as a professional cricketer. We won two trophies and should have completed a domestic one-day clean sweep. We also got to play against some of the best T20 players in the world in the Champions League in India which was an unforgettable experience. Okay, we also got relegated in the Championship but, having only survived by a handful of points in 2008 and with no Mushy in the team to bail us out, it was always going to be hard for us to stay up, especially with a new-look team. Of course relegation didn't go down well with some of the Sussex members, well those who only watched four-day cricket and thought T20 was a bit vulgar, but I didn't care to be honest. We loved winning trophies and I know the club were delighted. All

these finals and knockout games in front of big crowds, as well
as prize money, meant money was flowing into the coffers.
Everyone was a winner.

Physically, it was the hardest season I've ever experienced.
By the time we got back from the Champions League in
October I was so knackered that I didn't train or pick up
a bat for another eight weeks, which was unheard of for
me. At times I seemed to be surviving on adrenalin but the
job consumed me 24/7, as I knew it would. The intrusive
thoughts I'd suffered in Australia during the 2008/09 winter
had gone, for a while at least. I was just so focussed on being
a good captain and leading a successful team and on making
sure I performed my own role in the side as well as I could.

The squad we had and the template we used in T20 was
near perfect but we also got lucky with our overseas signings.
Yasir Arafat was developing into one of the best death bowlers
in world cricket and, although he was a bit of a punt, Dwayne
Smith, who joined us as a Kolpak registration, gave us that
X factor. Dwayne was a typically laid-back West Indian who
didn't say a lot, although he hid it well because he was as
passionate about doing well for Sussex as Mushtaq Ahmed.
When he arrived he'd just helped Delhi Daredevils win the
Indian Premier League and it was an ambition of his to try
and win two domestic T20 tournaments in the same year.

He was a dream to captain because he raised everyone
else's standards, including mine, most noticeably in the field.
It used to amuse me when he would amble into the ball from
the covers inviting batsmen to take his arm on. He would

literally jog towards the ball but in a split second he picked it up and had it in the wicketkeeper's gloves. I don't remember him throwing it even half a yard out of the keeper's reach, it was straight over the stumps, time after time. Some of the distances batsmen would be run out taking on his arm were frankly embarrassing. With Dwayne and lads like Rory Hamilton-Brown and Joe Gatting, who were both gun fielders as well, in the crucial positions square of the wicket the rest of us – and we didn't have any slouches in the field because it was an area of the game we really worked hard to improve – could relax because they weren't in those high-pressure positions. As a result we improved our own individual fielding performances.

Dwayne was the complete package – and he wasn't afraid of hard work. I remember him bowling 17 overs unchanged into the teeth of a howling game at Hove during one of the nine Championship appearances he made for us against Somerset. He was a tremendous athlete and when he came off with the bat, as he did in the T20 final to such spectacular effect, he could change the course of a game in the space of a few overs.

Somerset were our big rivals that season in one-day cricket. We put down a marker in late May when we chased 285 at Taunton to win in the Friends Provident Trophy. They had an experienced side and a strong batting unit with Marcus Trescothick, Craig Kieswetter, who made a century that day, and the Australian Justin Langer among others. But Murray Goodwin, Ed Joyce and I all scored half-centuries and we won with five balls to spare against a team previously unbeaten in one-day cricket that year. I still regard that as one of my best wins as Sussex captain. It gave us massive self-belief for the rest of our one-day campaign and by the end of the season Somerset must have been sick of the sight of us. That win was huge in terms of getting to the Friends Provident Final at Lord's instead of them, we also beat them in the final of the T20 and pipped them to the Pro40 title as well, after both teams had lost our last games of the season.

Leg-spinner Will Beer and wicketkeeper Ben Brown had become regulars in our one-day team, Chris Nash was starting to establish himself at the top of the order and show consistency and Joe Gatting played some important innings as well. We still had an experienced core with Murray, James Kirtley and Robin Martin-Jenkins, all of whom fed off the enthusiasm generated by the younger players in the same way I did. James and Robin knew their place wasn't guaranteed anymore so they raised their own games as a result just to stay in the side.

I had loads of bowling options. In some games I could have thrown the ball to all ten of the outfield players and be confident they could do a job for me. In T20 in particular this was very important. James, Yasir Arafat and I were nailed on for four overs each, which meant finding eight overs from guys like Smith, Beer, Martin-Jenkins, Nash and Rory Hamilton-Brown, the latter two more than capable of bowling decent spin on slow pitches like the ones we usually played on at Hove. If the three main bowlers could build pressure at one end, even if we didn't take wickets, it gave us control and meant batsmen had to attack the bowlers at the other end and play high-risk shots. With James and Yasir, we knew that if we had to defend between 30–40 runs in the last four overs, nine times out of ten we would win the game. Even if teams hurt us in the six overs of power play at the start I always felt that of the 14 remaining overs ten of them would be bowled well enough to give me control and help us drag things back.

Murray Goodwin struggled for runs in the Championship that year but he was so consistent in one-day cricket, particularly in T20 when his role was the hardest in the team. Batting at No.5 he might come in with two or three overs to go and be charged with helping us get another 30 or 40 runs on the board or occasionally he'd be in early on with us 15 for 3 and had to lead a rebuilding job. When he opened, he would set himself up to bat through the innings if possible. He had a fantastic knack of knowing exactly what the team required and invariably he would score runs when we needed them most.

I loved captaining in T20 and it also helped my bowling as well because every time I had the ball in my hand I was confident of doing my job. Mark Robinson, the coaching staff and I all had an input into team selection, although for most of the T20 campaign a settled team picked itself, but because of the nature of the game I had to think on my feet most of the time. For me, there was no wrong or right. It was almost as if I knew I couldn't make a mistake. If someone said to me "Why didn't you do this?" I had the same response every time. "Well, I could have done that but I decided to do this instead." Of course it helped that as a team we quickly built up momentum with a string of good results and luck tended to go our way, as it does when you are successful. If someone bowled a long hop and the batsman pulled it straight down a fielder's throat instead of it going a foot over his head for six you're a genius.

The margins are paper-thin in T20 but we gave ourselves a chance of success in 2009 because we had a really strong team ethic and a good mix of youth and experience. Although we lost our first game at Hampshire, we won four of the next six and then had a bit of good fortune when the floodlights failed during our home match against Kent and they finished two runs short of their Duckworth/Lewis adjusted target despite only losing one wicket. Two more victories ensured a home quarter-final against Warwickshire against whom we cobbled together 152 on a slow, low wicket and then bowled them out for 114, with Rory Hamilton-Brown's off breaks earning him four wickets.

For once, when we arrived at Edgbaston for finals day, we weren't favourites. The winners of the other semi between Kent and Somerset were but I felt there was almost more riding on the result of our semi-final with Northamptonshire, who were regarded as the weakest team of the four. Both finalists were guaranteed a place in the inaugural Champions League, a competition featuring the domestic T20 champions from around the world, in India at the end of the season. As well as being worth $6m to the winners, there was a hefty participation fee for each team while the exposure of playing against some of the best players in the world in the format would clearly help our development as a side. If you didn't think you would ever play international cricket or, as I felt at the time, you were unsure if you might represent your country again, taking part in the Champions League was the next best thing.

Knowing what was at stake against Northamptonshire also stopped us looking too far ahead, something we'd been guilty of in 2007 when everyone expected us and Lancashire to be in the final. All our energies were directed towards beating Northants and Murray Goodwin produced another gem of a knock, guiding us past their score of 136 with two balls to spare with an unbeaten 80 on a slow wicket. Two years earlier we'd played in the second semi-final but this time we were first on and I was worried that we'd expend a lot of nervous energy waiting around before we had to play the final. But having qualified for the Champions League visibly relaxed everyone and while some of the lads headed back to the hotel for a snooze I tried to figure out whether I could get to Molineux and back in time to see my beloved West Ham United in action against Wolves. Once I realised I couldn't I put my feet up and watched the football scores on the TV in the dressing room. I wasn't too bothered who we would be playing a few hours later.

Somerset captain Justin Langer tried it on at the toss, telling Sky's interviewer Nasser Hussain that all the pressure was on us, that we were favourites because we'd lost in the semis two years earlier when we were expected to win the tournament. I only found this out when I watched the TV highlights later. When we'd gone out to toss up I couldn't hear a word he'd said because of the crowd noise. Not that it would have bothered me much – stuff like that was water off a duck's back really. The ECB had given finals day a Wild West theme that year and when the teams came out before the start the Somerset lads looked so focussed, particularly Langer. In contrast, we couldn't stop pissing ourselves whilst Muz twirled his bat like some old gunslinger about to face down his enemy at the OK Corral while the PA system blared out the theme tune from *The High Chaparral*.

For the first half of our innings we scored at eight an over before Dwayne came in and played the match-winning hand with 59 off 26 balls, including three sixes and seven fours. That got us to 172 for 7 and on a pitch being used for the third time that day I felt it would be enough if we didn't do anything daft in the field. They started their reply well but when Rory Hamilton-Brown took a superbly-judged catch off a big top edge to get rid of Marcus Trescothick for 33 we had them. They imploded at the end, losing their last six wickets for five runs to hand us victory by 63 runs, the biggest winning margin in a final. Lifting that trophy and celebrating at Edgbaston with our supporters was right up there as a career highlight with England's World T20 success in 2010.

The Champions League, as I anticipated, was a brilliant experience. If only we'd been able to play our strongest team, I think we would have at least reached the second round. As it was, four of the triumphant Edgbaston XI were missing – Luke Wright, Murray Goodwin, Will Beer and myself, while Matt Prior was unavailable because of England commitments. I went down with Delhi belly the day before our first match against a strong New South Wales side, who went on to win the tournament. Phil Hughes and Moises Henriques, who six years later would be knocked out cold after a horrible collision with a team-mate on the outfield at Arundel during our T20 game against Surrey, both made half-centuries and we could only muster 95 for 8 in response on a very slow wicket.

Despite no local interest there was still a crowd of around 15,000 and the night we went to watch Delhi Daredevils play the stadium in Delhi was full to capacity. That was a real eye-opener for those lads who hadn't experienced international cricket. The atmosphere was fantastic and we were desperate to win our second match, against Eagles from South Africa, to prolong our involvement for another week. The pitch was again desperately slow and we were only defending 119 but 11 overs of spin from myself, Piyush Chawla and Rory Hamilton-Brown only cost us 45 runs and from being on course to win Eagles suddenly needed 12 off Yasir Arafat's last over and five from the last ball. Unfortunately, Ryan McLaren, the former Kent player, mowed it over deep mid-wicket for four which meant the game would be settled by a super over. We restricted them to nine runs from theirs but then Dwayne Smith and Rory Hamilton-Brown got a bit giddy and were bowled off the first two deliveries trying to muscle the ball over the boundary and that was that. The next day we were on our way home to England. The growth of the domestic competitions around the world such as the Indian Premier League and the Big Bash in Australia meant the Champions League only lasted for a couple more years which I felt was a shame because it was a really good concept. Fitting it into a packed schedule was always going to be difficult though.

We also retained our Pro40 title although to say the finale was a damp squib is a bit of an understatement. Ed Joyce, who had scored 546 runs in the Friends Provident Trophy, made 395 in this competition and James Kirtley took 14 wickets but they were our only players in the top 15 in the competition averages. Our success was, like the T20, built on a strong collective team effort. For instance, Joe Gatting made a crucial 99 not out when we defeated Yorkshire at Scarborough, one of six wins we enjoyed in our first seven matches, while Yasir Arafat bagged a hat-trick in the victory over Gloucestershire. Going into the final game of the season at New Road we knew a win over a Worcestershire side with nothing to play for would secure the title.

The problem was that by then, at the end of a very long and draining season, we were emotionally and physically cooked. We arrived straight from a loss at Trent Bridge to Nottinghamshire which confirmed our relegation in the Championship and we were dead on our feet. With what was at stake I thought we might summon up one more good performance but we batted feebly chasing a modest target of 215 and lost by 49 runs. All Somerset had to do now was beat Durham at Taunton and they were in control having posted 242 for 7. But as we looked on from the balcony at the live TV coverage on the big screen at New Road Durham squeezed out a victory with two balls to spare and 35 minutes after we thought we'd blown it we had somehow retained our title. Unfortunately, there was no helicopter landing on the outfield with the trophy, even though it had been in Bristol all day ready to head up or down the M5 depending on who were crowned champions. Instead, we sprayed champagne over each other and our supporters in the Worcester gloom and waved a sponsor's flag around. It was nice to win, of course, although the ending was a little anti-climactic.

The big disappointment of the summer was our poor performance in the Friends Provident Trophy Final at Lord's. A week before, we'd played Hampshire in the Pro40 at Arundel and beaten them by four runs and after all the spicy confrontations of previous years it was a relief to play them for once without an Adams–Warne ego-off as a distracting sideshow. We had Matt Prior back for the final and I had no hesitation in batting first. It was a warm, sunny late July day, not a damp early-September one, when the one-day final had traditionally been staged, and while Hampshire didn't have Warne they had Dominic Cork, who still possessed a temperament for the big stage and was very anxious to erase the disappointment of 2006 when we had beaten his Lancashire team in the final.

He took three wickets with the new ball, including our talisman Ed Joyce, and I knew our score of 219 for 9 was at least 30 runs short of being competitive. I finished with 92 not out but it came off 127 balls. I was caught between two stools. In hindsight I should probably have tried to attack towards the end but I only had the tail for company and I was also mindful that we had defended a small total three years earlier when we beat Lancashire. Hampshire eased to victory with more than ten overs to spare and my mood didn't improve when Murray Goodwin told me afterwards that we should have bowled first. He was in a minority of one with that assessment.

Still, we had delivered the best one-day season in Sussex's history – two titles, a money-spinning trip to India and a Lord's final. But those extra days playing in knockout games and, of course, preparing for them as well took their toll and was definitely a big factor in our failure to hang onto our first division status in the County Championship. We only won twice, both against Worcestershire who went down with us, and only two batsmen got a thousand runs – Chris Nash and yours truly, whose 152 at New Road was my biggest score in the Championship for three years.

Murray Goodwin had a very poor year by his standards. 344 of his 800 Championship runs came in one innings when he broke his own record, set against Leicestershire in 2003, for the highest score by a Sussex batsman, against Somerset at Taunton. It was very strange to see Muz struggling so much to bat against the red ball. He had his benefit that year which may have been a distraction but by contrast his form in one-day cricket was superbly consistent. Collectively, we didn't get enough runs, even though we only scored one fewer century than the champions Durham but our biggest fear in the post-Mushtaq era was quickly realised. We struggled to bowl teams out, particularly on the moribund pitches at Hove where our quickest bowler was Corey Collymore, who took 33 wickets but wasn't much above 80mph in pace.

Overseas players were a problem too. We were keen on Ashley Noffke, the Queensland fast bowler who could get the ball through at a decent pace, but he didn't want to commit himself for the whole season. My theory was that if we had the option we would have a gun overseas in the second half of the season, when trophies were being won and lost. At the start of it another Aussie, Damian Wright, came over fresh from helping Victoria win the Sheffield Shield. He had probably celebrated a little too much because he wasn't in the best physical shape when he arrived but he worked hard and I loved having him in the team. He had strong values and if someone stepped out of line in the dressing room he would not be afraid to tell them.

He only took five Championship wickets and would get exasperated trying to extract some life out of the dead wickets at Hove but I believe that overseas players don't necessarily need to make a massive impact on the field to prove their value and he was a case in point.

We hadn't started the season well but in a Friends Provident Trophy game at Durham in early May he bowled into the teeth of a gale when no one else wanted to take the responsibility and helped us to a victory that kick-started our one-day season.

Halfway through the summer we brought in a relatively unknown Indian leg-spinner called Piyush Chawla and he scored 102 not out batting at No.9 and took eight wickets on debut against Worcestershire at New Road. Not quite the new Mushy, but we thought we'd hit the jackpot with him. But when he came back for the last few games of the season, in the expectation that his wicket-taking ability might help us get the victory that would probably have kept us up, he didn't seem interested. We played Warwickshire at Hove and he was outbowled by Ant Botha, their unheralded left-arm spinner, while Ian Bell, in particular, and Jonathan Trott played him easily. He showed his inexperience but still finished as our leading wicket-taker with 36, which said a lot about our overall bowling performance that year.

Arguably the quickest bowler on our staff that year was a South African oddball with an Italian passport called Pepler Sandri, who we signed because he had an EU passport. He certainly had the fast bowler's physicality and in the tour match against Australia, which was another full-on occasion that season because it attracted full houses for each of the four days, he removed both their openers, Philip Hughes and Simon Katich. The trouble with Pepler was that he could only ever bowl in short spells – three overs was about his limit which wasn't a great deal of good to me. Against Australia, I remember pointing a finger to him after he'd just bowled an over, gesturing to make sure he came in quickly to stop their batsmen taking the single. He gave me two fingers back. Before I took umbrage he shouted out, "No, it's fine Yards.

I'm good for two more overs!" He was a bit strange. He rarely ate what the rest of us did, preferring to bring in his own stuff which mostly seemed to comprise of nuts and he ate at funny times, even getting up during the middle of the night to refuel. The Australians reckoned he didn't bowl as quickly as he looked. He was a nice lad, but we didn't bring him back for 2010.

We ended up needing to beat Nottinghamshire at Trent Bridge in the last game to have a chance of staying up but after Chris Nash had scored a century in our first-innings reply to their 328 we slumped from 156 for 3 to 243 all out and that was that. At least we didn't go down at Hove. I'm not sure how I would have reacted if the section of our membership who completely disregarded our achievements in one-day cricket had started to moan that we would have to prepare for our first season in Division Two since 2001.

We needed to do more rebuilding that winter. Age caught up with Jason Lewry, who retired at the end of the 2009 season after taking more than 600 wickets in first-class cricket for Sussex, and to try and improve our wicket-taking options we brought in Monty Panesar from Northamptonshire.

Sussex had developed a reputation over the previous few years of rehabilitating clearly talented players who had lost their way a bit, Mushy being the most obvious example. There were others and Monty probably fell into that bracket too. When he came to us he was a bit broken. He had started 2009 by helping James Anderson to save the Ashes Test in Cardiff with that heroic last-wicket stand but he was struggling to bowl as well as he could. Graeme Swann was already regarded as England's first choice spinner and by the end of that summer both Adil Rashid and James Tredwell were in front of him in the one-day pecking order as well. By joining us he was keen to embrace a new challenge and determined to get back to his best. So much so that a couple of weeks after he signed he went off, at his own expense, to play for Highveld Lions in South Africa for the winter.

Monty was certainly a challenge to captain. I was no longer in charge when the disciplinary problems which forced Sussex to get rid of him in 2013 emerged but with him everything was black and white. If he found the edge of the bat and the catch went down at slip he would get very frustrated. This happened quite frequently because of the speed Monty bowled at and the fact that at Hove the slips had to stand a lot closer than they would at other grounds because of the slow pitches.

He couldn't understand how, having done his bit, his team-mate couldn't back him up and take the catch, which in some cases was fair enough. When the edges came straight you would invariably grab it, but anything high or low demanded good reflexes. His attitude certainly had a detrimental effect on some of our younger players who soon became terrified of making a mistake. The trouble was, the more frustrated he got the quicker he bowled. At home, we had to encourage him to vary his pace on the slow Hove pitches and when he took that advice on board he did a job for us. On quicker surfaces or ones offering a bit of bounce he was outstanding.

Some of the team found Monty's occasional disappointment at their fallibility hard to take. And in fairness to him he did work on that aspect of his game as well as his batting during his time with Sussex. When he did get under a high catch he normally held it in those massive hands of his but there would be comical moments when you would see him trying to fix his eyes on a skier that would then drop to the ground a couple of yards from him, much to the amusement of the crowd if not necessarily the rest of us. If you saw him bat in the nets for the first time, you would think he was a top order player without a doubt. Unlike some tail-enders, he got into line and he wasn't scared of fast bowling. But then he would have what we called a 'Monty moment'. I remember he went in for me as night-watchman during a game in 2010 and got out for a duck playing a pull, which was a shot we'd seldom seen him attempt before even in the nets. As we crossed paths on the outfield he turned to me and said: "I should never have been night-watchman, I wasn't in the right frame of mind." Thanks Monty!

He certainly was an interesting character and at times provided the team with plenty of entertainment. Early in the summer of 2010 the club employed a new sports psychologist and at Derby one day Monty was sitting with our young batsman Michael Thornely when he started walking towards them. "He's coming to see us Mike," Monty shouted. "Because we need help!"

I'd shared a room with him on England Lions duty in India and we got on well but he was very introverted and kept himself to himself a lot of the time. A lot of people at Sussex, Mark Robinson and Mark Davis in particular, put in a lot of work during his first year with us, to get him back to something approaching his best, and it paid off. It's easily forgotten after the way Monty's Sussex career ended what a key role he played in making sure we went straight back up as second division winners in the Championship in 2010 when he took 52 wickets, and then the following year in helping to keep us in Division One.

Having got back into the England side, I missed seven of our Championship games in 2010. So did Luke Wright and Ed Joyce, who had a lot of injury and illness problems that summer, while Matt Prior was absent for nine matches. We won our first four games in Division Two then after losing two we won another four and clinched promotion and the title with a game to spare. For those of us with precious little exposure outside Division One the standard of cricket was something of a surprise, and not in a good way. In terms of the skill level of the individuals there wasn't a big difference but attitude-wise there was a discernible gulf. The application and mental strength teams showed in the first division was far superior.

In most games we knew that even if we just stayed in the match for the first couple of days the opposition would normally cave in. The standard of first-class cricket in some of the matches was poor and the defeatist attitude of some of our opponents was a real eye-opener. "What are you guys doing in Division Two, you're way too good?" We were asked that quite often during the summer. Even when Robin Martin-Jenkins retired halfway through the season, ironically when he was batting as well as he'd ever done for us, it barely stalled our progress. As I suspected, Corey Collymore, who took 57 wickets, was a real threat in the second division and Murray Goodwin and Chris Nash both topped 1,000 runs.

But it was a hard, hard season for me in sharp contrast to 2009. Flitting in and out of the side because of England commitments and coming back late to the squad because of the T20 World Cup wasn't easy. When I returned I should have been on top of the world but straight away I felt my authority was undermined simply because of my prolonged absence from the team. As vice-captain Murray Goodwin took over and did a great job but when I came back it didn't feel like my team anymore. The vibes weren't good and my decision-making lacked the clarity of the previous year. It didn't help that we made such a disappointing defence of our two one-day titles.

At first it looked as if nothing had changed from the end of the previous season as we won eight of our first nine games in the T20 qualifying stages. But then the team personnel altered a bit too much and we lost our momentum as quickly as we'd found it. The format had changed from ten group games to 16 and we won only once more and instead of securing a crucial home advantage we had to travel to Trent Bridge, where Nottinghamshire were very strong, in the quarter-finals. Even so, we should have won that game after restricting them to 141 for 9. We needed 36 off 21 balls with wickets in hand but then lost three wickets in the space of eight balls, including Murray Goodwin, and our reign was over. In the Clydesdale Bank 40 we finished second in the group but only the winners qualified for the semi-finals and we paid dearly for embarrassingly losing one of our early fixtures to the part-time Unicorns team at Hove.

The day after we went out of the T20 I spoke to Mark Robinson and offered to resign. Looking back, I'm sure I was suffering from depression then, even though I didn't know it at the time. I didn't want to do much other than play, train a bit and spend time with Karin and the children. I certainly wasn't in the mood to socialise. My world was closing in and little things had started to irritate me. The run-out incident with Murray Goodwin against Hampshire in the T20 a few weeks earlier ought to have been a warning that all was not right but I blithely ignored all the signs and carried on.

I was captain of Sussex. I couldn't show any signs of weakness. The boys were relying on me.

Robbo talked me out of it and for a couple of days at least I felt a bit better. I guess I just wanted some reassurance but the good mood didn't last very long. By the time I linked up with England again towards the end of the season for the one-day series against Pakistan everything had become a burden again. Playing for England. Playing for Sussex. Life really.

And on the morning of 22 September, in a hotel near Southampton, I caved in.

10

What's normal?

EVEN after I was diagnosed with depression and came home early from the 2011 World Cup I still thought it would be a matter of weeks or perhaps a couple of months before I'd feel normal again.

But what was normal?

To me, it would mean getting back into a familiar routine. Playing for and captaining Sussex, training and practising hard to try and be the best player I could and relaxing at home with Karin and the children.

What has actually happened to me in the five years since then could not be much further from the self-assessment I made back in the spring of 2011. Even at my lowest point in Sri Lanka, just before I came home from the World Cup, I never imagined for a moment that mental illness was something I would have to deal with for the rest of my life.

When I started to learn more about depression I was staggered to discover that mental illness, in one form or another, affects around 25% of the population. That's a lot of people who don't have a 'normal' life.

Everyone has bad thoughts and periods of self-doubt. But, as I explain to people when they ask me these days about my illness, those thoughts are just more intense with sufferers like me and sometimes crippling. I can hook onto a thought and cannot get rid of it. And the more I try to the more it takes over with a powerful intensity. I'll give you an example.

Late 2012. Sunday afternoon at home, watching football on TV while trying to assemble some flat-pack furniture.

And then it came into my head. On a night out I'd had in Brighton a few days earlier with a couple of mates I'd physically attacked someone. I thought I'd harmed someone.

One half of my brain was telling me this was a ridiculous notion, but I kept believing the other half. "Well how do you know you didn't?"

This went on day after day for the next four months, consuming me. Four months when all I could think about was the thought I had harmed someone.

Literally on a daily basis I'd scan the internet for news stories that had a link, even in the smallest way, to the thought in my head. I tried to remember all the different things that would help these thoughts go away, but the more I searched for the answers the more powerful the thoughts became.

All my fears seemed to be manifested in that one thought. Intrusive thoughts, which a specialist later told me was a form of OCD (Obsessive Compulsive Disorder), had started to define me, and every time I tried to push those feelings away the problem seemed to get worse.

Finally, I did what I should have done at the outset and sought help. Initially I spoke to Paul Khoury, the Sussex physiotherapist, and he referred me to a psychiatrist in Hove and on New Year's Eve 2012 I went to see her.

Even then, sitting in her consulting room, all I was after was more reassurance. She started by explaining that another of her patients had spent weeks going to the police station on a daily basis to confess to a hit and run accident that she hadn't committed.

The problem was I couldn't tell her that I had attacked someone or what happened because I had no evidence to prove the power of one thought. There was no proof. So I told her I thought I'd done something wrong but I didn't know what it was. My coping mechanism for the previous few weeks was to search high and low for evidence that I had committed an offence. This may seem strange but the thoughts were so powerful.

She straight away turned the situation around. "But what is the evidence that you *have* done something?" And, of course, there was none. Over a number of months, the intensity of my thoughts began to wane. I had clarity and in the next few months, although the thoughts were still there, they were much less powerful. All through those few months I could not totally focus on what I was actually doing. I would sometimes feel a sense of relief when the thought would not appear in my head for just a few minutes. The thoughts increased in intensity when they were supported by physical symptoms like shaking and sweating. These make the thoughts even more real. This period of my life really made me have total respect for the power of the mind. It was the scariest experience of my life. It also made me recognise the unbelievable skill of the psychotherapists who helped me challenge these thoughts and recognise them for exactly what they are – thoughts, but also how they take over and in some instances ruin lives.

I have never been a big drinker but since then, if I do go on a night out, I make sure I am with someone I trust implicitly, like Karin or a few of my old Sussex team-mates such as Chris Liddle, Ben Brown and Matt Prior. That way, I know I have someone I can rely on if I have a few drinks and later need reassuring with cold, hard facts: This is where we went. This is when we did this. This is how we got home. This is what you had to drink.

As I have mentioned earlier in the book, being totally honest about what happened to me during the World Cup was, in hindsight, probably an error of judgement. I could have put on a brave face, gone under the radar a bit, and began to get to grips with what was wrong with me and got treatment accordingly. After all, it had been three years since mental illness first started to affect me and I'd got through. I had learned to cope. When I had driven in the ground in tears, feeling like all I wanted to do was turn around and go back to bed, I'd struggled on and got on with it.

I was lucky in the months after March 2011 to have so many people supporting me. I know that thousands of people who have a mental illness suffer in silence. To this day, I don't know who funded my initial sessions with the specialists or paid for the medication I took, although I suspect it was the PCA (Professional Cricketers' Association) and in particular Kate Green, who do such a magnificent job looking after the welfare of the players. Lots of people took the time to write to me, either expressing their sympathy, wishing me well for the future or thanking me for highlighting the issues of mental health in the public domain. That was nice but, six weeks after returning home from the World Cup and preparing to return to action for Sussex, I still felt very fragile. I felt low and physically I was tired a lot. There were days when it was a struggle just to get out of bed. I never lay there all day, I just needed a bit of time to prepare myself.

Karin would know as soon as we woke up if it was going to be one of those days because my eyes would be glazed over and I would not be fully engaged to what she was saying. Those months cannot have been easy for her and I am so thankful for the love and support she gave me in so many ways. I know my behaviour scared her at times but she has always been pragmatic about things. When I came home from the World Cup in 2011 she had to ring both my parents and her own family to tell them what was happening, which was tough for her but was definitely something I couldn't have done at the time. But the more we talked about it, the better things were and I'm sure our marriage grew stronger as a result. One thing

I always tried to do was not let it affect my relationship with our kids. Syenna was five and Raffy aged three in 2011 and a couple of years later we had our third child, Marley. All they knew was that on some days it was Mummy who was taking them to the swings or dropping them off at school or nursery because Daddy was at home.

I didn't deliberately try to avoid people I didn't know but I didn't really want to talk about my illness and I did develop something of a sixth sense when I knew the conversation was heading in that direction. When people told me they knew what I was going through because they had similar experiences I struggled sometimes to remain composed. Of course I was sympathetic and I could never be rude to anyone but at that stage I didn't really understand what was happening to me and why, so how could anyone else, other than a specialist, know? And I certainly never felt in a position to diagnose other people's problems. I never hid away. I couldn't really. I was a professional sportsman with a profile, at least in Sussex and in the game of cricket, but I was very wary when strangers, or even people I knew, approached me throughout most of 2011.

Explaining what had happened to my parents, and particularly my Mum, was tough. I don't see my Dad much as he has built a new life for himself in Wales, but Mum was living back in Hastings and we saw her quite regularly when she came to see the grandchildren. Karin outlined what had been happening when I came home from the World Cup but Mum struggled to understand, which was not surprising. All she wanted to do was help but she did not know how to. I imagine she thought, "He's achieved his dreams. He's played for his country so why hasn't he enjoyed it?" That's probably what a lot of people believed. I can assure you now that is all I ever wanted to do. I remember listening to Talksport radio a couple of days after I got back and one of the presenters was pontificating on the subject, the gist being how could anyone who is playing for their country and being paid well to do it be depressed? Surely it's people living on the street, sleeping in doorways or struggling to make ends meet who should be depressed?

Of course circumstances can play a part, but because you choose to do certain things in your life or career does not guarantee immunity against mental illness. I also think it's harder for people from older generations to understand but people you or I know, whether they be family members or friends, probably suffered from depression in the past but couldn't work out what was wrong with them. They suffered in silence. Fortunately, I didn't have to.

My biggest issue was being judged as a bad person by other people or thinking I was in some ways inadequate myself. Not just worrying about others but setting unbelievably high standards for myself, which were sometimes not even achievable.

The more I learned about my illness the clearer things became. Although I had some fantastic times playing for England, by the end of the summer of 2010 I was trapped in a cycle that I could not break. I wasn't enjoying playing for my country because I was depressed, even though I didn't know it at the time. This made me feel guilty and in some ways worthless because this had been my dream and other people's dream for me and I should have been embracing and enjoying every aspect of the experience of representing my country. This made me feel like I was a bad person which made me feel depressed and sad. I wanted nothing more than to enjoy every moment of what I was doing but the illness was stopping me.

It came to a head in 2011, but there had been times when I played for Sussex, going back many years before then, when I experienced similar feelings. By 2008 I was definitely not socialising as much with my team-mates as I had done earlier in my career, which suggested, to me anyway, that I wasn't a good team man or a good person. That made me feel low.

But did it go even further back than that? Are there incidents growing up that have an effect on your mental health later in life?

The cognitive therapy sessions I undertook helped me get a proper understanding of what had happened to me. They helped change the way I felt: the pessimistic thoughts, the harsh evaluations I had of myself and the unrealistic goals I had set. They also helped me prioritise what was important in life. During those sessions I was asked to look back on little incidents in my life that I still remembered clearly because they had brought on feelings of anxiety. One of the obvious questions was whether my parents splitting up when I was 16 may have sparked such feelings at the time but I never believed that they did.

Most of the incidents I was asked to recall concerned my anxiousness about whether I fitted in or felt I belonged in certain situations. Every time I went into a new environment I was worried whether I would be accepted or not. I remember the first time I went on an England age group squad training camp when I was 13 or 14 years old. I got out of bed one morning without doing much to my hair and it looked a bit of a mess. For the rest of the camp the other players took the mickey out of my 'bed hair'. It was something really trivial but they kept on and on at me about it for the rest of the camp. I remember right at the end of the camp bursting into tears because it had affected me so much. Silly really, but I still recall it with the utmost clarity and that incident would play back in my mind. Could this affect how I viewed different environments? Possibly? Now, because of the therapy I have received, I am in a position to understand why I may be anxious in certain situations and actually they have nothing to do with that situation, it may just be bringing up feelings from the past.

It's amazing to think now, given the torment of the previous few months, but when I started to pick up the threads of my life and career again in the early weeks of the 2011 season I still thought I might play for England again.

It makes me laugh now thinking I could have played for England again. I was partly in denial of the illness and I was holding onto an ambition that had always been with me. Looking back now, I knew I was not good enough in 50-over cricket and that cricket moves on very quickly. Players can quickly be forgotten.

Instead, I spent the remaining five years of my career trying to prove myself as a cricketer all over again, as if I was a young player just starting out.

Being diagnosed with depression had drained me of all my confidence as a player. And I never got it back.

11

Proving myself again

FOR two or three years after 2008 depression left me teetering on the edge. Edge of what? A black hole, a cliff face. You can use any metaphor you like really. I think you get the idea.

I was someone who was very intense in some ways, more laid back in others but always willing to push himself, always happier when I was striving to be better. I had always over-analysed things and until my diagnosis I saw that as one of my strengths as a person. I was always searching for a solution so I could improve my performances on the cricket field and even in life in general I suppose. Then, in 2010, I pushed myself too far. And instead of stopping myself just short of the metaphorical cliff face I tumbled over it.

And, in terms of cricket, it was bloody hard to get back to anywhere like where I had been during the good days. Seasons such as 2005 and 2006, when the runs and wickets came freely and suddenly I wasn't just Mike Yardy of Sussex I was Mike Yardy of Sussex and England.

The 2009 summer was when I captained my county to two trophies and enjoyed myself and felt more fulfilled than any other of my 16 seasons as a professional. When I was so full of confidence in my decision making, so confident of what my team could achieve under my leadership and so infused with self-belief.

Then I crashed. My confidence evaporated and for the last four years of my career, from 2011 onwards, I almost felt like a young player when I became a professional back in 2000, constantly trying to prove himself all over again. That's why I retired when I was 34, at the end of the 2015 season. The majority of county batsmen these days can normally retain form and fitness until they are 38 or 39. Some – Mark Ramprakash and Marcus Trescothick spring to mind – go on scoring runs and producing match-winning performances for their teams into their fifth decade.

There was a time when I thought I'd be like that. In early 2010 I was in the gym one day, thinking about my career so far. I had started at Sussex in 2000 and realised that I was halfway through my career – another ten years to go. In the end I only made it to five and there were a lot of occasions during that period when I probably didn't deserve my place in the Sussex team based purely on form.

Technically, I was still a good player post-2011. But mentally, I was nowhere near as strong as I had been. The first diagnosis of depression drained me of confidence and I never really got it back, apart from on a handful of occasions before 2015 and then again once I'd announced I would be retiring at the end of that season. In those few weeks between the announcement and my final game against Yorkshire I did what most players did in those circumstances. I stripped it all away and got into the battle again. But for most of the time I spent the latter part of my career constantly seeking reassurance either from close friends and family or the management at Sussex, in particular head coach Mark Robinson who was unbelievably supportive all through my career especially during the really tough times. I had lost my way, whereas before the illness I had a kind of deep ingrained confidence about myself as a cricketer and a captain. I did sometimes seek advice but would always be confident of making my own decisions. That was definitely the case in 2009, my first year as captain when we won two trophies.

Throughout my career I have always thrived on the challenge, no matter how hard it was. In a game situation I always preferred a scenario when I had to walk out to bat and the scoreboard showed something like 20 for 3, the skies were an ominous shade of grey, the wicket was doing a bit and the bowlers were on top. That brought out the mongrel in me. Two innings which I played in 2013 spring to mind as probably the best I produced in the last third of my career.

We played Derbyshire at Derby in mid-May and not surprisingly for that venue at that time of the season it was hard work for the batsmen. We bowled them out for 223 but then found ourselves 109 for 5 with Mark Footitt, their very good left-armer, threatening to run riot. For me, that was the perfect time to be batting. Bring it on. Initially at least, every run had to be chiselled out. Chris Jordan joined me and played very maturely for his 92 but by the time I was last man out for 153 – my first hundred of the season – we had taken the total to 401 and were on our way to a nine-wicket victory.

I loved it. I was proud of both my shot selection and the fierce concentration I had shown for long periods when it was bloody hard work.

A few weeks later we were in Taunton playing Somerset. Normally, the wicket is as flat as anything there. In recent seasons the groundsman has tended to leave some grass on the wicket but once that had burnt off it became the usual road. I walked out with us 8 for 2 with Steve Kirby, their flame-haired and occasionally hot-headed opening bowler, and the promising youngster Craig Overton moving it all over the oche and extracting some proper bounce, which was also unusual for Taunton. Lovely. All I needed to find was a partner to take it back to their bowlers. On this occasion it was Matt Machan, someone who I really enjoyed batting and playing with, and together we put on 275 of which I contributed 156 including my first hundred runs from 99 balls, which was pretty quick progress for me. Once I had done the hard bit I made sure I went on and helped us to another victory, again by nine wickets.

I always felt, when my team needed it most, that I stood up. It was the same when I was bowling, particularly in white-ball cricket. If the pitch was flat it gave me licence to be more aggressive and also a touch experimental, to really think hard as to how I could tempt the batsman into playing a false shot with changes of pace or the angle at the crease from where I delivered the ball. Captaincy really brought out the resilient side in me too, particularly in 2009. I think the other players in the Sussex team quickly realised that year that if there was a battle to be fought their skipper would not be taking a backward step at any time. I always felt Rory Hamilton-Brown had the same mentality as me. Ben Brown is very similar to Rory and myself. He loves to rally round the cause.

I always really enjoyed playing Surrey, especially at The Oval. We were invariably up against international players and certainly in the first half of my career we played against cricketers I looked up to and aspired to be like. We were always the underdogs, the upstarts up against the big-city boys. I don't think it's any coincidence that I always did well against them, even though it was Yorkshire against whom I scored more hundreds than any of the other 17 counties. Again, they loved a scrap and more often than not boasted an attack with two or three international bowlers. It was usually the same against Lancashire too. They always wanted a fight and when you played them, particularly at Old Trafford or Liverpool, you knew that they wouldn't give an inch. Tough, hard cricket that was relentless but if you came out on top victory didn't half mean a lot more.

Those sorts of challenges seemed to be fewer and farther between in the last five years of my career. Or perhaps they were there but I was struggling mentally to meet them head on as I had done before 2010. And the problem for me, particularly towards the end, was that when I didn't have to really show my competitive edge I struggled to summon up any motivation at all.

I have only scored one double hundred in my career. As a comparison, Murray Goodwin managed it eight times for Sussex and also lodged two triple hundreds. That inability to cash in, to be able to walk out with the scoreboard showing 200 for 1, the bowlers going through the motions and the pitch as flat as a pancake, and make a big score consistently eluded me. The opportunity to grind a team into the dust and get easy runs just did not motivate me. It was probably my biggest weakness.

I had nothing but admiration for players who could do that. The best players would relish the battle and the tough times just as I did. But they also understood that if you kept doing the hard work then eventually it would become much easier, that the bowlers would tire, the fielders would switch off and runs could be scored fairly easily and you would probably only get out if you made a bad error of judgement. Murray was the best player I played with at doing that with Ed Joyce, who succeeded me as captain in 2012, not far behind. They were remorseless once the hard work had been done.

I was never much of a sledger during my career. I'd have the odd word now and then but I would always have a go at opponents who only seemed to score runs when the going was easy, who would fatten their average but who, when the battle was really on, would take a step backwards. Sure, they would still try to compete with the opposition bowlers but they wouldn't fully embrace the struggle.

In terms of the captaincy of Sussex, I told Mark Robinson during 2011 that if, at any time, he thought it wasn't beneficial for me to carry on he could make a change with my blessing. I was missing a lot of cricket at that time as I came to terms with my diagnosis but he was fantastically supportive, as he always had been. I'm not sure how I would have reacted had I not been captain but I never thought I could not do the job and I was grateful for Sussex's continued support. I knew that at some stage in the future I probably couldn't be captain and a senior player as well as trying to come to terms with mental illness, but it was reassuring to know that when I decided to step down the decision could be made by me on my terms.

For only the fourth time since 1999, we ended 2011 without a trophy. But it was still a relatively good season for Sussex. We reached the knockout stages in both one-day competitions and fifth place in Division One represented our best finish in the Championship since we won the last of our three titles back in 2007. Ed Joyce and Chris Nash established themselves as one of the best opening partnerships in the country, Murray Goodwin scored 1,372 runs – only Marcus Trescothick finished with more in the Championship – and our young left-hander Luke Wells came through, with his 103 against Durham helping us to one of our six wins. And with Matt

Prior now a pillar of the successful England team, Ben Brown established himself as first-choice wicketkeeper-batsmen.

For the first time since the arrival of Mushtaq Ahmed, we didn't rely on overseas players either. James Anyon, who we'd signed from Warwickshire, finished with 55 wickets and on the lively Hove wickets he was a real handful. Jimmy became a good friend of mine off the pitch. Like me, he loved a scrap and he didn't mind doing the hard work: bowling into the wind or bowling long spells so the other seamers could get a breather. And he was very quick when he slipped himself, one of the quickest bowlers on the circuit at that time.

Amjad Khan had his best season since joining us from Kent with 39 wickets and Monty Panesar had a magnificent summer. Not only did he take 69 wickets but he bowled 750 overs in the Championship and was rarely collared by the opposition. It meant we could bowl four seamers and gave whoever was in charge – and we had three captains that season in myself, Ed Joyce and Murray Goodwin – terrific options.

By the middle of 2011 we had some good momentum in all formats but then Luke Wright, who had been struggling for a while with a knee injury, was forced to go under the surgeon's knife and didn't play again all season. His last match for us was on 15 July and, in one-day cricket in particular, we naturally missed him badly. Any side would of course. By then he was developing into an outstanding one-day batsman and while the knee problem meant he bowled fewer overs he could always be relied upon with the ball if we needed him.

The T20 competition group stages once again comprised of 16 group matches, the same as 2010 and, between spells in and out of the team as I continued to have treatment and rest, I played in six of them, but I could sense that the elongated qualifying format was definitely having an effect on the quality of the cricket itself.

By 2011 basic mistakes in T20 matches were becoming more commonplace. The game itself only lasts three hours of course but there is a real intensity to them which demands total concentration, whether you're in the field as captain or a player or even in the dugout waiting to bat, where you would basically be discussing tactics almost ball by ball with the rest of the team and the coaching staff. But when the number of qualifying matches went up the quality of the cricket in a lot of games went down, not that the watching public probably noticed – or, I guess, cared.

The audience profile at T20 has, of course, always been a lot different from the County Championship which attracted the stereotypical cricket fan – usually male, white and middle aged – who would happily sit and watch 100 overs a day and be totally absorbed by it. And although the behaviour at T20 occasionally got a bit like the crowds you see at football matches, even at its most extreme I never sensed the same tribal mentality I experienced at Upton Park watching West Ham play though I remember a game at Hove where a few West Ham fans and their Brighton counterparts had a scrap at the Cromwell Road end and the police had to be called.

I realise that for the majority of the paying public T20 is not primarily about the quality of the cricket, more the spectacle. If there was the odd dropped catch or mis-field it was almost always greeted with pantomime laughing or booing but as a player, and certainly when I was captain of the side, I hated to hear people in the crowd jeering one of my team-mates for a mistake.

Winding down afterwards was always difficult as well, especially if I was captain. If it had been an eventful game, I would often be lying in bed churning over what happened until three or four o'clock in the morning. A few hours later we would be practising for a Championship fixture and be expected to perform the following day in a totally different format. No wonder, if it was a green seamer, batsmen often struggled to summon up the energy or mental strength to dig in. Instead, you would sometimes take the other option and play a few more shots than you normally would and see how it went.

At Hove, we won five of our eight T20 group games and one was abandoned without a ball bowled. We tended to play on low, slow pitches, sometimes using the same wicket two or even three times, and we'd push the boundaries back as far as we could. With our battery of slow bowlers, such as Monty Panesar, Ollie Rayner, Chris Nash and myself we forced batsmen onto the defensive, nudging and nurdling but never really accelerating even if they kept wickets in hand. We bowled Somerset out for 90, restricted Gloucestershire to 121 and Glamorgan 132, chasing successfully on all three occasions, and when the wickets were a bit easier to bat on we made over 170 against both Surrey and Essex, which tended to be a winning score at Hove and in those two instances was. Our left-armer Chris Liddle was developing into an excellent one-day bowler and took 20 wickets in T20 that year while the returning Rana Naved, complete with hair-weave, was an excellent foil because of his skill at reverse-swing. Between them they took 37 wickets and we finished second in the group to secure a home quarter-final.

The problem was, by the time we played Lancashire at Hove it had been three weeks since our last T20 match. We hadn't forgotten how to play the game of course, or what worked best for us particularly at Hove, but the momentum we'd built up in qualifying just was not there. On the morning of the game Luke Wright failed a fitness test and without him we were always going to find it difficult. Having said that, a chase of 153 ought to have been achieved but Lou Vincent was caught behind first ball – an incident which became increasingly significant when the match-fixing scandal broke – and although Chris Nash made 31, Rana 34 and I contributed 24 off 24 balls, it wasn't enough. That defeat was certainly the single biggest disappointment of the season.

Poor quality matches weren't just prevalent in T20 cricket either. In the middle of August, we were on a gruelling run of fixtures. We played Yorkshire at Scarborough in the Championship and although I was thrilled with my own contribution – hundreds in both innings – it had taken it out of me physically. The following day we played them in the

CB40 competition – which that season comprised of 12 group games – and lost only our second match out of ten by 35 runs. It wasn't likely to affect our chances of progressing through to the quarter-finals but after getting back home in the early hours of Monday morning there was hardly any time to rest, never mind prepare properly, before the next CB40 game at home to Kent the following day.

I had been instrumental in bringing Lou Vincent to Sussex. When I had played for Central Districts in New Zealand in their T20 competition in 2010 he had scored a really attractive half-century against us. Later in the tournament I saw him make a century in a televised game and when I met up with him and the rest of his team-mates before another match a few days later he asked me if we were interested in bringing him to Sussex. We needed an attacking batsman for one-day cricket and he was a fine player with an excellent international and domestic record. I contacted Mark Robinson who was as keen as me and we sorted out a deal for Lou to come to Sussex in 2011.

I have never met anyone in life, never mind cricket, whose mood could swing as dramatically as Lou Vincent. Generally, he was an energetic personality but he was all over the place a lot of the time. The life and soul one minute, the next someone who would hardly say a word.

The first thing to say about that infamous Kent game – where it later emerged that both Lou and our Pakistan all-rounder Naveed Arif had basically performed to the order of Indian bookmakers – was that the standard of cricket from both teams was pretty poor. As I mentioned, we'd come into the game after a long road trip and were knackered and Kent were in the same boat. I remember dropping a straightforward slip catch while Kent's Martin van Jaarsveld, who was one of the best fielders on the circuit in the cordon, spilled catches off two successive balls. The wicket was a bit like the two teams – lacking in life – but we felt we could chase a target of 217 in 40 overs comfortably enough, especially as the incentive for us was a home quarter-final if we won.

We got off to an excellent start thanks to Ed Joyce and Chris Nash, who put on 76 for the first wicket in 12 overs. Ed was caught behind off Darren Stevens for 20 but, under the lights, the ball was coming onto the bat a bit quicker as the late-August dew settled and we were still in an excellent position.

Lou came in at No.3 and was run out for a single by van Jaarsveld in the covers after facing seven balls. I don't even remember what our reaction was on the balcony at the time but I do vividly recall that when he came back to the dressing room he was more animated that normal, in a frantic state of mind almost. Before he'd even got his pads off he was quizzing the rest of us quite incessantly. "What do you reckon guys? Was there a run there?" In those circumstances nearly everyone I played with would have gone back inside, thrown their pads off and maybe smashed their bat against the nearest hard surface in frustration. We'd got used to Lou's ups and downs by then and at the time I and everyone else considered his reaction to be fairly routine behaviour for him. But when the match-fixing allegations came out I remember thinking it had all seemed to be a bit forced, stage-managed if you like.

Naveed was also implemented in the same game, which had attracted $14m worth of bets on the exchanges in the Far East and India, more than double the amount normally wagered for a televised game. Earlier, he'd been expensive with the ball, his six overs going for 41 runs. I don't remember thinking anything was awry that day with his bowling, although he was expensive in the context of the match, but there had been occasions during that season when Ben Brown, who would be stood next to me at wicketkeeper, and I would have a quiet laugh with each other when Arif would bowl an unplayable delivery followed by one that scuttled two feet down leg side with poor old Browny waving it to the boundary for four byes. Of course, the last thing we thought at the time was that it was in any way dodgy.

When he came into bat we need 81 off 18 overs but had lost six wickets. Not a great position for us but by no means hopeless. Naveed batted at No.9 in our one-day team but he was better than a tail-ender. Earlier in the season he made a Championship century against Lancashire at Hove and he was more than capable of giving it a whack. In one-day cricket he tended to go on the attack from the start and would invariably get out cheaply. Mark Robinson was always banging on about it to him. "You've got the ability, but you must bat time. Bat time. Bat time." And that night he did, scoring 11 runs off 29 balls. Okay, the match situation wasn't great but that was taking it to extremes.

We lost the game but afterwards and the following day there was no inquest. No one mentioned Arif's go-slow or Lou's reaction when he was run out. We just got on with preparing for the next game.

Rumours of match-fixing in both that game and the T20 quarter-final against Lancashire began circulating a few months later but it would be nearly three years before the matter was finally put to bed. Lou Vincent admitted to 18 breaches of anti-corruption rules and received a lifetime ban from the ECB, applicable to cricket all over the world. Naveed Arif received the same punishment, having admitted to six breaches a few weeks before Lou had been banned in July 2014.

The whole thing had hung over Sussex for three years. Having initially decided nothing untoward had happened, the ECB's anti-corruption unit eventually investigated both matches again and all of us who had played in the games were interviewed. I mentioned in my chat about Lou's strange reaction to getting out and Arif's untypical go-slow when he had batted. I would imagine they must have colluded many times during that season, although if it went on in the dressing room I never saw it. They surely wouldn't have been that daft.

In May 2014, my mobile phone rang. I didn't answer it at the time but when I picked up the message later on I was surprised to hear Lou's voice on the other end of the line. "Hi Yards. Look, you probably don't want to talk to me but I'd like to apologise for what happened and the grief it caused you and the club. I will ring you back tomorrow."

He never did and, to be honest, I doubt if I would have spoken to him. I felt very angry when the allegations first surfaced and three years on my emotions on the issue were still pretty raw. At the time of the Kent game I was really struggling to cope with my diagnosis of depression and learning to live with mental illness. On the pitch I was scrapping hard to be a good captain and to contribute to the team. It was one of the toughest periods of my life. I am sure, like most of my team-mates, I would have gone home after that game deeply disappointed that we had lost and analysed my own performance wondering what I could have done better to affect the result positively for Sussex. Meanwhile, there were two blokes out there basically playing for the opposition. The thought of that is still pretty painful even now.

I have played all over the world for England and had a 16-year career in the county game and never once was I approached about performing badly to deliberately affect the result of a match. There are some people who think it's endemic in the county game because of the sheer volume of matches which are shown live on TV, particularly in one-day tournaments, and not just for domestic audiences but throughout the subcontinent and India in particular, where there are 70,000 bookies operating underground in the country because though the practice is illegal there. I'm not so sure. I think most county cricketers are pretty similar in the way they approach their profession, too wrapped up in their own game to concern themselves too much with external influences. Maybe I'm being naïve, but I don't think so.

In terms of captaincy, I went into 2012 hoping it would be something of a fresh start and initially I did well. In our second Championship game at Liverpool against Lancashire I made 110 as we enjoyed a ten-wicket win and when we played them again at Hove a few weeks later, in a match ravaged by rain, I scored 63 as we chased bonus points when the game finally began on the final day. But they were the only scores above 20 I got in my first ten Championship innings and I finished the season with a pretty underwhelming 574 runs at 24.95. As well as the responsibility of captaincy I was still trying to come fully to terms with my illness. Eighteen months on from my initial diagnosis I certainly had a clearer understanding of depression but learning to live with it on a day to day basis was still a learning process at that stage. With all that going on I wasn't devoting enough time to my batting, to trying to rediscover the methods that had brought me success before. Something had to give.

After we'd lost heavily to Middlesex at Lord's at the beginning of June, where I'd contributed scores of 8 and 10, I approached Mark Robinson and told him I didn't think I could carry on as captain. He gave me a few days off and we worked something out because he wanted me to be in charge for the T20 competition, which was just about to start, but I went away thinking that it was only a matter of time before we would have the same conversation. I couldn't see my situation or how I felt changing in the short or long term.

The T20 qualifying campaign went well and I was pleased with my own performances, particularly with the ball where my economy rate was a miserly 4.31. The number of group-stage fixtures had sensibly been reduced to ten and although the south section was, as always, extremely competitive, we had a good, well-balanced side fortified by the muscular hitting of another New Zealander, Scott Styris. We won six of our matches and three of the others were abandoned because of rain which meant we sailed into the quarter-finals. Matt Prior was smashing it all over the place and finished with more than 400 runs while Luke Wright and Chris Nash were consistent performers with the bat too.

Results started picking up in the Championship as well. After winning just one of our first eight games we won four on the bounce at home. It was a tough summer not just for me but our other batsmen as well. We didn't collect maximum batting points once and only scored more than 350 on three occasions but we had a habit of winning the arse-nippers, such as the game against Durham at Arundel when Steve Magoffin and James Anyon got us to a modest target of 94 having been 73 for 8 after Mags had earlier taken nine wickets for us.

Steve was totally unheralded when he joined us that year, but proved to be – and still is – one of the best overseas bowlers Sussex have ever had. He had a good record in Australia but had relatively little experience of English conditions, apart from brief spells with Worcestershire and Surrey. So no one was expecting too much but he took 57 wickets that season at just 20.05 and developed into one of the best new-ball bowlers in the Championship. He was a skipper's dream really. He could bowl long spells, kept himself supremely fit and was a great team man. I only wish I'd been able to captain him on more occasions than I did.

At the end of July, we played Nottinghamshire at Trent Bridge and I had another poor game with the bat, scoring 0 in the first innings and 3 in the second, after Chris Nash and Ed Joyce had put on 216 to effectively save the game on the fourth day. I came out to bat with about ten minutes left before I was going to shake hands with Chris Read on a draw, one of those everything to lose and nothing to gain situations. I pulled a length ball from Harry Gurney straight to mid-wicket and walked off thinking and probably knowing that, as far as captaincy was concerned, my race was run.

There had been an incident earlier in the game which told me the same. At the end of a session, when Notts had put us under the pump a bit in the field, Mark Robinson had told the boys he had been pleased with the way we'd stuck at it. For probably the only occasion in my time as captain – I'm struggling to remember any other instances – I stood up and contradicted the coach's assessment. "I'm sorry Robbo, for me that wasn't good enough by us." My outburst was a manifestation of an increasing frustration at my inability to make any sort of contribution in terms of consistent runs.

I wanted to tell Robbo on the way back from Trent Bridge, but because it would have meant Steve Magoffin driving home on his own I had to wait until the following morning after a long, sleepless night wondering whether I'd made the right decision. I felt no differently in the morning, though, and this time Robbo made no attempt to change my mind. He did, however, come up with a compromise of sorts. He wanted me to carry on as T20 captain and I was delighted to do that. Having guided us to finals day for the third time I cannot deny that the prospect of picking up the trophy for the second time as my last act as Sussex captain was an exciting one.

A few days before the announcement we had smashed Gloucestershire at Hove in the T20 quarter-final thanks to a stunning innings from Scott Styris, one of the best I have ever seen in my career. We were in a decent position – 100 for 3 in the 12th over having earlier been 7 for 2 – when he went in and smashed a century off just 37 balls, the third-quickest in the history of the format.

Scott was a fantastic competitor and had brutal hitting power when he was in the mood. He was built like a light-heavyweight boxer and on nights like that it looked like his bat was as light as a toothpick in his hands. For one of the few occasions on a cricket field I felt sorry for a member of the opposition when he flayed James Fuller for 38 in an over, including 20 off one legitimate delivery – a beamer that went for six, a front-foot no-ball he hit to the boundary and another six off the subsequent free hit. Our score of 230 for 4 was never going to be overhauled and we went into finals day, which was being held in Cardiff for the first time, full of confidence.

Ed Joyce had been appointed as my four-day successor and that was the natural choice, especially with Murray Goodwin struggling for form, so much so that at the end of the season he wasn't offered a new contract and moved to Glamorgan. Regardless of the rights or wrongs of the decision to let one of the best players in Sussex's history go, even though his 40th birthday was fast approaching, it was personally a relief not to have to be part of the decision to release him. With 49 first-class hundreds and over 15,000 runs Murray had been a magnificent servant for the county and someone I still regard as a friend. I was delighted when Sussex brought him back in 2016 to be batting coach. I think it's a job he will be ideally suited to.

Ed celebrated his elevation in the ranks with a century in a victory over Worcestershire at Hove. I made 33 and felt a lot better having spent a bit more time on my batting in the nets. I then contributed 89, my highest score since the second game of the season, in a win over Middlesex in a low-scoring match at Hove. Our fourth successive home success had left us with leaders Warwickshire in our sights and for the first three days of our next match, against Somerset at Taunton, we got ourselves into a winning position. On the final afternoon we needed 49 more runs with five wickets in hand when it started to rain. A couple of times it looked as if the clouds would clear but eventually play was abandoned and our opportunity to go top of the table, albeit by a single point, with two games to go disappeared. It had been a frustrating few hours and did little for our state of mind as we headed across the Severn Bridge that evening to prepare for T20 finals day. We got to Cardiff quite late and as we were first on the next day against Yorkshire our preparation was far from ideal.

But we had developed a successful formula that season and we started the game well. I opened the bowling with Scott

Styris and my four overs only cost 23 runs while Scott bustled in and picked up three wickets, including Joe Root for 11, and Yorkshire were 36 for 3 in the sixth over. Unfortunately, that was as good as it got for us. Jonny Bairstow played a gem of an innings with 68 off 45 balls and put on 82 in ten overs with the South African David Miller.

We didn't need to be told that their total of 172 for 8 was the highest at Cardiff for 15 months but, with one notable exception, we batted poorly in reply. Luke Wright (3) and Matt Prior (2) went cheaply but Chris Nash and Murray Goodwin seemed to be rebuilding nicely, taking us to 55 for 2 in the ninth over. But after Murray was out for 15 we imploded – there is no other word for it really – with no one else getting into double figures. Nashy carried his bat and contributed 80 off 58 balls, including 24 runs alone from Dilscoops, but no one else could match his ingenuity or hang around long enough with him.

We finished on 136 for 8 and by the time Hampshire were beating Yorkshire by ten runs in the final I was back at home watching on TV, my captaincy career over in the most low-key way.

Having played a game more than Warwickshire, our failure to beat Somerset effectively scuppered our chances of winning the Championship and it was no surprise really that we lost our last two games as our momentum stalled. But there was still the Clydesdale Bank 40 to play for and despite losing four of our 12 matches to rain we bounced back to beat Kent at Canterbury in our final group game, two days after the disappointment in Cardiff, after Luke Wright smashed a century and Matt Prior helped him put on 152 for the second wicket as we won with ten overs to spare and clinched a home semi-final against Hampshire.

A year earlier, at the same stage of the competition (and without either Lou Vincent or Naveed Arif) we had performed badly against Surrey in a rain-affected game at The Oval which we lost by 71 runs, not helped by four dropped catches. At Hove, though, we were confident against anyone but, as had been the case in the T20 semi-final, we didn't bat well enough. Instead of Chris Nash it was Luke Wright who played the lone hand this time with 122 out of our total of 219 for 8. The next highest score was Matt Prior's 28 and we knew on a flat pitch with a quick outfield it was unlikely to be enough. And so it turned out. Michael Carberry and James Vince smashed 129 for the first wicket and Hampshire won with seven overs to spare.

It had been a nearly sort of season for us and when it was all over I finally had the opportunity to take stock on my spell as captain. I'm certainly very proud of what the team achieved under me. In 2009 we won two trophies, including the T20 title for the first time, and the following year we bounced back immediately from relegation in the Championship to win promotion back to Division One as champions and, in 2011, came fifth in our first season in the top flight again. In one-day cricket we were certainly a much stronger unit than the one I'd inherited.

I'm very proud of my win ratio in T20 cricket of 70 per cent as well. Captaincy brought out a lot of admirable qualities in me and I'd like to think that I made us as tough a team to play against as had been the case under my predecessor Chris Adams.

But, as I was to discover in what turned out to be the last three years of my career, when I wasn't in charge there was definitely a dulling of my own competitive edge. And as I continued to get to grips with my illness I knew that was unlikely to return. Soon, it would be time to start thinking about a life after cricket.

12

Winding down

I NEEDED to have something to motivate me to perform for Sussex at the start of the 2013 season and, daft as it may sound now, that driver was the prospect, albeit the very remote one, that I might play for England again. It had been two years since I exited the World Cup in tears but I still felt I had something to offer in T20 cricket. There was a World Cup coming in 2014 in Bangladesh and I didn't see why I wouldn't at least be in the frame if I played well in 2013, particularly in white-ball cricket. That thought sustained me throughout the year and even during the first part of 2014, until I suffered one of the worst injuries of my career – a torn bicep – and I realised that England had moved on and that it was probably the beginning of the end for me at Sussex too. As I spent a frustrating three months recovering from surgery I started to give serious consideration to what I was going to do after cricket and, more importantly, I put some concrete plans in place.

Although England was a distant dream it definitely motivated me in 2013. I didn't miss the captaincy and without the added responsibility of leadership I was able to form much closer friendships with some of the younger players in the Sussex squad. I hadn't ignored them when I was in charge but with so much else to do there wasn't really time to develop relationships, apart from those long hours on the motorway coming back from an away game when I would occasionally have a good chat with someone before inevitably I would fall asleep on the back seat.

As a result, I am proud to call guys like Chris Liddle, Ben Brown and Will Beer good friends now. I was an usher when Chris got married and I still socialise with them quite a bit even though I have retired. It's funny because I bowled a lot of overs with Will operating at the other end over the years, particularly in one-day cricket, but I didn't really know what made him tick. Now, on my return to the ranks, I had the opportunity to put that right and enjoyed making solid friendships which will hopefully last until we're all old and grey and sitting in the deckchairs at the County Ground moaning that the game isn't the same as it was in our day!

In the Championship, 2013 was the most productive season I'd had since 2011. I scored 834 runs at 34.88 and twice passed 150. As I mentioned earlier, I was still motivated by tough match situations. Both big scores came in difficult conditions against Derbyshire and Somerset but, to be honest, there weren't too many other days like that during the summer. I enjoyed the season and my one-day record of 357 runs and 16 wickets was decent enough. I tried to bat with a bit more freedom but, not for the first time in my Sussex career, the team were unable to sustain a challenge for honours on more than one front.

Ed Joyce seemed to thrive on the twin responsibilities of captaincy and being a senior batsman alongside myself and Chris Nash. He scored 1,118 Championship runs, including a double hundred against Nottinghamshire at Trent Bridge, and was out three times in the 90s. We were unbeaten in our first ten Championship games as Steve Magoffin and our new signing Chris Jordan formed one of the best opening pairs in the country and we led the table after I'd contributed 156 to our win over Somerset at Taunton. But we just couldn't get going in the T20. We beat Middlesex in our second game but that was our only victory in ten group-stage matches which was embarrassing really given the talent in our squad. We did slightly better in the Royal London One-Day Cup with three wins but our poor form in limited-overs cricket, combined with a hectic mid-season schedule, drained us physically and mentally. We lost two Championship games in a row against Derbyshire and Middlesex and although we ended with a victory over the new champions Durham at Hove, our first win at home in the Championship for 13 months and one which enabled us to climb to third in the final table, we might as well have finished sixth or seventh as far as I was concerned.

Halfway through the season Mark Robinson and I decided to try and look after my mental health a bit more. We were due to play a one-day floodlit game against Nottinghamshire at Trent Bridge, followed the next day by a four-day Championship match. Players hate those scenarios. Win or lose, it can be very hard to switch off after a floodlit game and then prepare properly for a totally different challenge a few hours later. We had no chance of qualifying for the knockout stages and Mark knew that I really struggled to unwind after a day-nighter and that insomnia could sometimes lead to episodes of depression for me. I was left out for a T20 against Middlesex at Hove a few weeks later as well, for the same reasons, but I didn't feel it helped. I still needed the regular rhythm and routine of playing and practice to be at my best.

I felt I had made a solid contribution to the 2013 season and towards the end of the summer I approached the club about giving me a new contract which would take me up to the end of 2015. I felt my performances had earned it and the club agreed, verbally at least, with the promise that they would dot the i's and cross the t's once the campaign was over.

I didn't think anything more about it until the final game of the season against Durham when I had my worst experience since I came off during the Middlesex T20 game more than two years earlier. If you look at the pattern of my illness, when I have had really bad moments, it has usually come at the end or beginning of the season. Those are the times when I have often struggled. At the start of the summer I would always have massive expectations of myself in terms of performance and if I didn't deliver straight away I could quickly make a huge deal of it and start fearing that my place in the team was already under threat.

Similarly, at the end of the season if I looked back and didn't feel I had done myself justice I would experience those same feelings of angst and disappointment. Add in general fatigue which we all experienced at the end of a long summer and things would be worse. And if we weren't fighting for honours in late August and September I would struggle to motivate myself. I was never excited, as a lot of players were, by the prospect of finishing in third place and picking up a few extra quid in prize money at the end of the season. It was all or nothing for me. Always has been.

We batted first against Durham and I got a horrible pearoller from Graham Onions and was out for a duck. The following morning, I couldn't get out of bed. "You'd better ring Robbo," I told Karin. "I don't think I can do this anymore." It was another very scary incident. It was the first time in more than two years that I'd missed a day's cricket. I wasn't seeing a therapist at the time because, after the incident the previous winter when I was convinced I'd attacked someone, I felt I had things under control. Where the hell had this come from? At least now I knew a little more about how to deal with the bad days. After a day's rest my next cogent thought was 'what can we do to stop this happening again?' You start to work things out.

Once the season was over and there was still nothing definite on the table from Sussex in terms of a contract I started to fret again. I trusted the club, but there was definitely a feeling in the back of my mind that they might renege on what we had agreed after what happened during the Durham match.

Mark Robinson and the Sussex physio Paul Khoury came to my house to discuss things and they insisted that Karin was also there. They just wanted to reassure me that the club had things put in place and they told me they thought it was important that we all worked together. I felt the club always tried to help me with my illness. In the early stages after my diagnosis they trusted me to make the calls regarding my mental health and at this meeting we all agreed that somethings needed to be implemented to try and help me further. My fitness levels were monitored as regularly as fat tests, as a drop in standards were sometimes a sign that I was starting to not take care of myself as much as I should – that I might be getting into a dark place.

Broadly speaking, it was pretty similar to all the contracts I had signed before but for the first time there were a couple of caveats. Broadly speaking, it was pretty similar to all the contracts I had signed before but for the first time there were a couple of caveats, including extra monitoring of my fat test scores.

Even though I have always been a big lad my fat test results have always been pretty low. I tend to carry any extra weight around my middle and not in my upper arms or legs, which are the areas of a cricketer's body that do the most work. If I was in good shape my test score would generally be around

65 but if I was out of condition it would go up to around 82–83. As a comparison, someone like Matt Prior was always in unbelievably good shape but his tests would often be close to 78 and if he had a few days away from the gym and regular training it could shoot up to between 120–130. We agreed that mine had to stay below 70 as part of my new agreement.

Most cricketers these days, particularly bowlers, are proper athletes with toned physiques. As a batsman you can probably get away with being a little bit heavier. I have never been depressed over my body shape. I have always been stocky, going back to when I was growing up in Hastings, but sometimes I would look at myself in the mirror, when I was putting on the pounds, and feel awful about what I was staring at. That happened a few times after I began to suffer from mental illness. I was told when I started to take medication that it would either make me lose weight or put the pounds on.

Another side-effect of my mental illness was a tendancy to eat more when I was depressed. I know, not least because of my family genes, that I was never going to be someone with an unbelievably athletic body and chiselled physique. People might accuse me of using it as an excuse for the times when I did look heavy but I learned to manage it and actually used it as a motivation, to prove to people that I could keep myself in good enough condition to cope with the physical demands of professional cricket and still keep contributing in terms of runs and wickets.

More often than not I would walk down to Withdean Sports Centre, near to our new house in Brighton, and do a fitness workout before joining the rest of the squad at the ground for our scheduled gym session. There are many players I shared a dressing room with in my career who couldn't wait to tell you that they were doing a bit extra in the gym, whether it be upper-body weights, core work or a cardio session. For me it had become a matter of course. But the big difference was that for most of the guys who did extra the results were there to see when they looked at themselves in the mirror. I never really had that luxury and it did become a bit of a bugbear of mine. I had to accept that if I didn't do extra then my physique and fitness levels would invariably suffer.

The club did sweeten the pill slightly by awarding me a benefit in 2014. Financially, of course, it was a massive thing for me and my family but, as you might expect, certain aspects of running a benefit are quite stressful. For starters, the prospect of speaking in front of hundreds of people, many of whom were total strangers, brought me out in a cold sweat, initially at least. It's not something I am at all comfortable with and, as far as cricketers are concerned, I don't think I'm alone.

I remember writing my first speech and then feeling a bit of a fraud when I repeated bits of it at subsequent events because there were people there who might have heard my first effort. And at my launch event at Brighton & Hove Albion's Amex Stadium I ended up feeling slightly uncomfortable when they played a video at the start show-reeling my career highlights with England and Sussex. Honestly, I'd have been more comfortable if they'd put together a montage of dropped catches, deliveries of mine being hit out of the ground or my stumps being splattered.

But I cannot lie. Even I enjoy occasionally being in the limelight. I guess deep down, even the most introverted of us like to be feted now and again, to be told that actually you're pretty good. And the more dinners, lunches and speeches I did the better I got at speaking to an audience. I still preferred it when we had the question and answer format but by the end my speeches were pretty much off the cuff efforts, with a few notes for guidance in front of me. And the experience has certainly helped me since I retired, when I have had to do presentations based around my university coursework. I still get nervous but I do feel more comfortable than I did because I know I can do it.

Karin was on my committee and worked tirelessly to organise things along with my chairman Ian Poysden and people like Andy Crompton and Alan Smith. Alan is probably most well known for his successful spell as manager of Crystal Palace but when he left football he became an agent, looking after the likes of Alec Stewart, Matt Prior and myself. Alan became more than my representative though. When I was suffering badly in 2010 and 2011 with depression he was in regular touch. I will always be grateful for the help they gave me during my benefit year and continue to offer. More importantly, they have become good friends as well.

Cricketers' benefits have got a bad press over the past few years, unfairly in my opinion. The general public see the sums that players, particularly those who play or have played international cricket, can rake in and wonder if it's fair that on top of their substantial playing earnings they get a hefty bonus for effectively being the star of the show at a few dinners or golf days, a bonus that until last year even evaded the clutches of the Inland Revenue as well. I don't think it's as black and white as that. I know players who have given away vast sums from their benefit, without publicity, to charities or other causes close to their heart. I was proud during 2014 to support the work of the mental health charity Mind. The average county pro doesn't make a fortune from playing the game. They certainly don't earn enough that once they stop they don't have to think about another career. You're a long time retired and I always say to people that don't agree with the benefit system the answer is simple. Don't support the beneficiary.

I had no excuse not to get stuck into organising my events in 2014 after I was sidelined with the worst injury of my career. It happened in a T20 game against Glamorgan in Cardiff at the end of May. I slipped as I came in to bowl and landed awkwardly but got up and didn't think anything more about it. But as I went to deliver the next ball I stopped in my delivery stride and when the ball did come out it had the same speed and velocity as if I was bowling a rose petal and was duly smashed high into the Cardiff night sky for six. Then I felt this excruciating pain in my left arm and had to be helped off the field.

Initially, the physios at Sussex thought it might heal naturally and I would be able to play again in a few weeks and I was desperate to make a quick return. We had won two of our first three games in the T20 and were starting to play well. The physios thought I had torn off about 40% of the bicep but when it didn't get any better and it was decided I would have an operation the surgeon found it was more like 90%; the muscle was literally hanging on to the tendon. I was to be out of action for three months. We lost that game to Glamorgan and only won four more times in the group stages and didn't reach the quarter-finals.

It was a huge blow to me because I had just started to run into a bit of form. Against Lancashire at Old Trafford, opponents and a venue I always enjoyed, I outscored all ten of my team-mates to make my first hundred for ten months as I batted for over six hours before being run out for 139. I had been bowling well in T20 and Sussex's season was starting to pick up as well. Those three months really dragged and although there weren't too many days when I struggled to get out of bed I hated not playing. I'd never been out for that period of time before and I struggled. I watched the occasional session of play at Hove when I went in for treatment or to start my rehabilitation but in the end I was very grateful for the distraction of helping to organise my benefit.

And when I did come back I wasn't ready. I thought I was, even though I had just one net session at full pelt before going off to play a second-team match against Surrey at Purley. I scored a hundred in that game and felt as though I'd never been away. But then I played in another second-team match, this time against Somerset at the Blackstone Academy Ground, and flayed around like a novice, scoring 9 and 16 without any control or thought at all. I made my Championship return in the final home match against Lancashire, batting down the order at No.6. I was going okay on 14 until Chris Jordan ran me out, a suitably low-key finale to a disappointing season. Quite how I thought I could return after such a long period out and pick up the threads again straight away I still can't fathom out now. In terms of my goal-setting I had been totally unrealistic again. I finished the season with 361 runs at an average of 27.77 in the Championship and five T20 wickets from the three games I played in before the injury. Mitigating circumstances obviously, but I was hardly finishing my career with a flourish.

During the winter of 2013/14 I had started to give serious thought to what I was going to do next. I'd actually had my first discussion with Chichester University about joining their sports and exercise psychology course in 2013 and was planning to start full-time the following year. But the more I thought about it the more I realised it was unrealistic to expect I could combine full-time study with professional cricket. I suppose I imagined being able to sneak off to the deckchairs at Hove for a couple of hours and bury my head in a book when I wasn't required by the team but eventually I knew that it would be impossible to do both properly.

Instead, I spent 2014 doing an access course, which is a bit like the Open University in that you learn at home for a year and get used to the routine and demands of studying. Initially, my results and feedback were pretty good but it was winter and I didn't have cricket to worry about. When we reported back early in 2015 to start preparing for the new season my results fell away because I couldn't keep up with the coursework. I was starting to have to email lecturers to tell them I would be taking a hit on my marks because I hadn't been able to finish an essay or a certain piece of work.

I had a decision to make. I certainly did not want to give up a course I was enjoying and had committed to. As usual I thought I could get through it, even though there weren't suddenly 36 hours in a day instead of 24. Fortunately, the marks in your first year of a full-time course did not count towards your final degree but something had to give and early in the 2015 season two incidents convinced me that it was time to stop playing cricket.

I was actually looking forward to the new season. I felt the team had missed me in 2014. Although we bombed in the T20 and failed to reach the knockout stages for the second successive year, and only won three games in the Royal London Cup, we'd finished the Championship campaign strongly, winning four of our last six games to come third behind the new champions Yorkshire. My own contributions, thanks mainly to the injury, had been fairly modest, but I still felt I could score runs and take wickets across all formats.

But I knew the end wasn't far away, although as we headed off to Dubai for pre-season I had not given really serious thought to finishing in 2015. I was trying really hard to enjoy it more. For instance, I made a conscious effort in

Dubai to try and immerse myself in the city itself rather than confining myself to the hotel so occasionally I would go off for a walk around the shops or on the beach. And sometimes I'd manage a whole 30 minutes before starting to think about the next game, the next day's practice or something else related to cricket. The only time I could really enjoy my cricket was when I was playing well, and those days had become increasingly few and far between in 2013 and 2014.

When we got back to England our first competitive game was a friendly against Leeds/Bradford MCCU, the students who would turn up in early April and invariably be cannon fodder for county batsmen eager to get themselves into some sort of nick and, if it had the added bonus of being a first-class fixture, buttress their average against the prospect of tougher times once the serious stuff started. The first day was standard for early April at Hove – dry fortunately, but cold and grey and pretty cheerless all round with only the Sussex diehards, who saw it as a badge of honour to see the first ball of the season bowled, dotted around the ground.

I went out to bat and it was as if someone had flicked a switch on in my head.

"I fucking hate this. I'd rather be doing something else – anything else in fact."

Playing entirely from memory, I actually made our top score of 88 but I just could not be bothered with it, even when it was announced during my innings that I'd scored my 10,000th first-class run. Some pretty scary thoughts have entered my head during 15 years as a cricketer but never one like that. It was a warning sign but once again I chose to ignore it.

There was another a few days later. There were a few injuries about in the squad ahead of our first Championship game against Hampshire at the Rose Bowl and Mark Robinson had asked me if I would open the innings if it was required. Normally it would have been the sort of situation that got my competitive juices flowing, a challenge I would relish. The Rose Bowl, early April, facing the new ball on a green seamer? Bring it on! Except not this time. "Yeah, whatever" was my underwhelming response.

It got worse. Much worse.

We were staying in the same hotel in Southampton where I'd broken down while with England in 2010. I genuinely believe that going back there for the first time since then triggered bad memories, even subconsciously. I was okay for the first couple of days, even though I was out for 6 after we'd won the toss and batted first. Fortunately, Ben Brown and Luke Wright played brilliantly to get us up to a score of 444 as the pitch flattened out and then we dismissed them for 231 to put ourselves in a strong position.

On the second evening I had a drink and a bite to eat with a couple of the lads in the bar and I could sense their excitement at the position we had got ourselves in to start the season with a win. But when I went to bed I felt on edge and I barely slept a wink. At 5am I woke up and knew straight away that I was struggling. A couple of hours later I was on the phone to Karin in tears. Groundhog day.

Karin phoned Mark Robinson who came to see me. I should have gone home there and then, of course I should have. But once again my over-riding instinct was that I didn't want to let anyone down. Grit, determination – the qualities I had in spades, especially in times of adversity, got me to the Rose Bowl. Only Robbo knew how bad I felt, the other players were oblivious. I was out for a duck, but oddly that didn't make me feel any worse. My head was in a daze. I just walked off the ground thinking this was so unfair because people would judge me on the fact that I was out first ball without knowing the full picture, that I'd been awake most of the night in that horrible place again.

I packed up my gear and did go home. We went on to achieve an excellent victory but I can't say it made me feel any better. That was the case in a lot of matches during the latter part of my career, when depression was stalking me, whether it was with Sussex or England. I just could not enjoy the good times.

It was my worst moment since the Durham game at the end of 2013 and, as they had done then, the club explained my absence against Hampshire as illness, which I guess in a way it was.

Sussex had been honest about the incident against Middlesex in 2011 because I'd walked off during the middle of a game but I was quite happy that they didn't give any details about the subsequent two breakdowns, even though on both occasions I knew people would be sympathetic. I'll be honest. I wanted a rest from the scrutiny that I'd have had to face if I'd admitted the real reason why I had missed more cricket. You didn't have to be Einstein to work it out though. A lot of people around the club knew my mental issues had resurfaced, especially the other players.

I felt better a few days later and went to see Robbo and told him I would happily give up Championship cricket if they wanted me to and have my contract adjusted accordingly so I could concentrate on one-day cricket. But they were against that idea. The coaching staff still thought I had something to offer and after a few days of rest I stirred myself to go again, as it turned out for the last time.

The T20 was coming up and I thought we had a good chance of doing well so that was a motivation. In the Championship I made my return against Middlesex on the worst Hove pitch I've ever played on and scored the only half-century in the game. This time the toughness of the situation did motivate me.

I have never been hit as often as I was in that match as balls spat off a normal length and struck me on the helmet, the gloves and the stomach. I was covered in bruises but they didn't seem to hurt. We lost the game but I felt rejuvenated and, for a while at least, thoughts of retirement were put to the back of my mind.

It didn't last long. We started the T20 campaign well and had some good early victories, particularly one against Somerset at Taunton. I had been bowling well but during that game I felt a bad twinge in my calf during my spell. I carried on but the physio diagnosed a grade two tear, which normally means six to eight weeks out. six to eight weeks? Superman Yards was back in a week.

I missed our next Championship game, when we beat Warwickshire by one wicket on another minefield at Hove, but I then returned for the rump of the T20 qualifying campaign. The physio jokingly referred to the injury as a slow twitch because it didn't affect me as much as I was an endurance-based athlete rather than a sprinter. But it was still stupidity on my part. Perhaps I realised that there might not be too many more opportunities so I had better make the most of them. Whatever the reason, I'd be hobbling around in the outfield like a carthorse. It was a good job I hadn't lost my reflexes in the slips. I took six catches in that Middlesex game and was quite happy to stand at slip, nattering away to Ben Brown to my left.

The team's results in T20 were consistently good and we put ourselves in a position to qualify for the quarter-finals and get a home game as well. But I was putting myself under a lot of strain physically because of the injury and it was definitely one of the reasons why my bowling suffered as a result. But it wasn't the main one. After only playing three T20 games in 2014 I had spent quite a bit of time the following winter in the nets working on different deliveries. In the past one of my main strengths had been an ability to replicate what I did in practice in a match situation pretty much straight away. But now that self-belief had gone. I couldn't re-invent myself anymore.

It came to a head in mid-July during a T20 game against Hampshire at Hove. I opened the bowling but my four overs went for 43 runs. By then I was down as low as No.9 in the order so hardly able to make up for a poor spell of bowling with the bat. A few days earlier I had spoken to Karin about retiring at the end of the season. Me talking about giving up the game was a speech she'd heard many time before so I'm not sure whether she thought this was going to be any different.

After that Hampshire game I came off the field and found Mark Robinson. This time he didn't try and talk me around. I think, like me, he knew this was the end. He was probably relieved for me. I know I was.

But the competitive juices still flowed. When I returned after the calf injury I was mightily pissed off to lose my place in the Championship team. I had played on some terrible pitches early in the season and did as well as anyone so when I was left out for the game against Warwickshire at Edgbaston at the end of June, having declared myself fit, it felt like a kick in the teeth.

I think I have always been good at evaluating my own performance and being honest with myself but this felt harsh. Craig Cachopa had struggled in the early weeks of the season but he was brought back in my place for a few games and hardly did any better. It was nothing personal against Craig, who I think has got a great future ahead of him at Sussex, but I felt it sent out the wrong message.

Still, there was the T20 quarter-final against Northamptonshire to look forward to.

The south group was as competitive as ever with just five points covering the top five counties. We squeezed into second place thanks to a no-result in our final match at The Oval after rain washed out our game and the rest of the final round of matches. Northants were a very useful T20 side, and had unexpectedly won the tournament in 2012, but at Hove we always fancied our chances against anyone.

I think you all know what happened next.

All I can say is that for a few moments after David Willey had hit me for 34 runs – five sixes and a boundary – in a single over I thought he'd taken me for six sixes! To be fair, Willey crashed all of our bowlers around that night as he scored a sensational hundred off just 41 balls, having earlier taken three wickets as well. I walked off at the end of the over thinking 'that went for a few' but it wasn't until halfway through the next over, when I had a look at the scoreboard, that I realised how many 'a few' actually was and, as I tried to work it out between deliveries, I genuinely thought he'd done a Garry Sobers on me.

I can remember on one hand the number of times I conceded 20 or more in an over in T20. Statistics have never been a motivator for me but I am very proud that over a ten-year career in the format my overall economy rate was less than seven runs an over. They even survived that final onslaught but it was a very painful experience for me. What it did do though was reaffirm my belief that it was time to go because if there was ever an over when I needed to come up with something different that was it. I still had those deliveries in my locker, but by then I completely lacked the confidence to bowl them. It wasn't the first time I'd bowled into the wind with the shortest boundaries to protect but in the past I'd have come up with something, even if it was a ball Willey could have only squeezed out for a single so I could get the other batsman on strike. Now, I had nothing new to offer.

So instead of my Sussex T20 career ending in champagne-soaked reverie at Edgbaston with us winning the trophy for the second time we had to listen to Northants bawling out their team song on the other side of the dressing-room wall. I did congratulate Willey on his innings afterwards but another long night followed before I finally nodded off at 5am. And before you ask, no I have never seen a replay of that over so I don't know that the ball that only went for four was only a few inches short of clearing the rope!

Once my decision to retire had been announced by the club I had no regrets but I was very determined that my last act as a Sussex cricketer after 15 years would not be that over I bowled to David Willey. I went back into the second team and got some form back, scoring 131 against Glamorgan and 90 against Hampshire. I didn't mind being back in the seconds to be honest, it was almost as if the previous 15 years hadn't happened. I was back in a time of my career when the only way to prove yourself, if you weren't in the team, was to get runs or take wickets in the second team. The instructions that had been drummed into me by Peter Moores on the first day I went to Sussex to be a professional cricketer remained the same.

I was finally relaxed and enjoying myself. I could have let things just fizzle out but those runs gave me the confidence I needed to perform when I got back into the team at the beginning of August when we played Middlesex at Lord's and I scored 70 in the first innings in a game we lost. We then beat Worcestershire at New Road and with three games to go we had probably an even chance of staying up. The trouble was that two of those matches were against the champions-elect Yorkshire.

At Hove, in contrast to most of the Championship wickets we'd played on, the pitch was flat and their score of 494 put us under severe pressure. I came in at 139 for 3 which soon became 175 for 4 and Yorkshire thought they had us but batting felt as natural and comfortable to me as it had done at any time in the last few years and, with a cause to battle for as well, I was in my element. I made 124, my first hundred since May 2014 and first at Hove since September 2007.

By then I was still practising but training a lot less and I wish I had adopted that regime more in the last few years of my career. What's the phrase? Train smart? Who knows. If I'd been able to think that way more often I might have played a bit longer and, more importantly, enjoyed it and it is frustrating that I only seriously began to look at the way I prepared once I knew that not long down the line I wouldn't have to worry about it at all. Instead, it was always my belief that I had to make up for a lack of talent with hard work. I thought it was a sure-fire way of making me a better player.

Matt Prior was the player whose training regime I wish I could have emulated. When he came back to play for Sussex he would work out with an intensity most of the rest of us struggled to match. I could, but then long after Matt had finished I would still be at it, working my nuts off. I knew that one hour of high-intensity work was better than three hours at a slower pace. I was told it so many times. I just couldn't work that way. That was me. My only concession to impending retirement was that, in those last few weeks of my career, I didn't really care what I looked like when I went out to bat.

Before, even though I used to have big trigger movements, I always tried to get in positions where I looked good. Now, all I was focussed on was being as comfortable as I could at the crease. See ball, hit ball, run if you have to. That's batting in essence isn't it?

My last game at Hove was against Somerset, who were just above us in the table. With Yorkshire to come away in the final match we certainly needed to avoid defeat and another good batting wicket was prepared with the hope that our seamers, boosted by the return of Chris Jordan, might give us the edge. I went in on the first day at 136 for 4 and that quickly became 171 for 6 but I felt good and got to stumps 60 not out. It was during days like that, right at the end, that brought home why Sussex was always the perfect club for someone like me. We always liked to think we could compete with anyone. Mark Robinson always used to say we punched above our weight but that wasn't a phrase I was comfortable with.

We didn't just want to compete. We wanted to stand up, puff our chest out and tell the opposition that we can beat you as well. Next morning the runs flowed quite quickly. Suddenly, I looked up at the board and I was on 98. Tim

Groenewald obligingly bowled one down the leg side which I tickled to the boundary and that was it. Helmet off but no wild celebration (I couldn't break the habit of a lifetime) as the Hove crowd stood as one to applaud me. A special moment.

And a few minutes later there was this awful feeling of frustration. With Chris Jordan going well at the other end and the Somerset bowling starting to get ragged I really thought I could go big, to finish at home in style. The adrenalin was flowing which is the only explanation I can think of for thinking I was Chris Gayle as I was caught for 104 on the boundary trying to clear long off. Another standing ovation when I walked off and then a third one at the end of the game, which finished in a rain-affected draw. Karin and the kids were there and they all rushed onto the outfield as I walked off. I think they were more emotional than I was. All I could think was we had to beat Yorkshire at Headingley. We had to stay up. I don't even think I cleared my locker out that night.

The best bit about my last two games was the respect the opposition showed me. All the Somerset lads applauded and congratulated me when I made my hundred and then on the last day of my career at Headingley I went out to bat with the Yorkshire lads, several of whom I had played alongside for England, forming a guard of honour as I walked to the crease. Adil Rashid even came up to me as I was about to take guard to ask me not to walk off too quickly when I was out so he had the opportunity to shake my hand.

The situation was pretty precarious. The wicket did a bit and replying to Yorkshire's 251 we were in trouble at 70 for

5. But not for the first time that year Ben Brown played a great innings and I contributed 70 off 81 balls, quick progress by my standards but, as I mentioned, I was batting with real freedom by then. I was demob happy. We restricted their lead to three runs then bowled them out for 305; 309 to win and loads of time left to get the victory, which we knew by then we needed with Hampshire beating Nottinghamshire.

You probably know the rest. We were soon in trouble at 61 for 5 but Browny came in again and we started to put a few runs on the board. We took our stand up to 81 from 20 overs when Tim Bresnan had me caught in the slips for 41 by Alex Lees. I started to walk off and this time the Yorkshire lads ran from all corners to shake my hand. A lovely touch by them but I was utterly deflated. An hour or so later we had been bowled out for 208 and were heading into the second division.

I think I was chucking my kit into the dressing-room bin at the time the last wicket fell. Apart from my treasured county cap, a helmet, which I plan to get framed alongside my England one, a bat and a few shirts, which I'd promised to collectors, it all went. It had been a horrible end for the team but I was happy that, on a personal level, I'd finished in the way I'd wanted to. I made the journey back down the M1 with Browny, Matt Machan and Chris Liddle, who was on the phone to his agent most of the time anticipating that, like me, he had played his last game for Sussex. I really felt for Browny. He'd had a magnificent season, keeping wicket superbly and finishing with 1,031 Championship runs – the first Sussex wicketkeeper since Matt Prior in 2003 to top

1,000 runs (and Matt didn't keep in all the games that season). He deserved better but I have no doubt Sussex will challenge very strongly for an immediate return to the top flight and if Ben continues to make the progress he showed in 2015 he is a genuine contender for England involvement at some level at some time in the future.

The day after the final game the club staged a tribute dinner for Matt Prior and I which was a lovely gesture on their part but it was a bit subdued all the same given that we had gone down the previous day. Earlier, I learned that Lidds, who had become one of my best friends, had, as he anticipated, been released by Sussex. It brought home to me the fragility of what we do, or in my case did. One minute you have a career, an income, a future and the next it can disappear. I wanted to retire, and did so on my own terms as so many of my former team-mates, like James Kirtley, Jason Lewry and Richard Montgomerie, were able to, but at 31 Lidds still felt he could play first-class cricket. Earlier that day I drove past a coffee shop in Hove where he and his wife Charlotte were sitting outside, no doubt discussing the future. Normally I would have stopped and the kids, who adored them, could have said hello but it didn't feel right. What could I have said? I was delighted when he got fixed up at Gloucestershire later in the year.

So why did I keep the bat? Not sure really. I'm not a great one for mementos and memorabilia but I guess I might get it framed one day or let one of the boys play with it in the back garden. I certainly didn't hang on to it with the intention of ever using it again. I genuinely believed that if I'd wanted to I could have carried on, whether it was with Sussex or somewhere else. But, seven months after I retired, I will be honest – I can't think of anything worse. I had a great career but I'm pleased it's over. I really won't miss playing at all.

13

New beginnings

W HEN I walked off the field at Headingley on my last day as a professional cricketer in September 2015 I really felt a sense of desperate disappointment that the one last challenge I had set myself after announcing that I was going to retire – to help Sussex stay in the first division – had not been achieved, but over the next few months, particularly when I sat down to work on this book and review my career, I was content with what I'd achieved and excited and, I must admit, a little nervous about what lay ahead. I was comfortable with my decision to retire but there was some apprehension too. Cricket had been my life since I walked out of William Parker School nearly 20 years ago and now I would have to find a way of prospering in the real world.

I was never academically gifted. At 16 I knew I had no chance of going to university. It was cricket or nothing. Well, not nothing obviously. I would have done something and probably played for Hastings Priory at weekends. Thankfully the coaches in the junior set-up at Sussex saw something they could work with. Now, in 2016, I find myself back in the classroom again, almost as if the last 20 years or so had not happened. Here I am, a 36-year-old learning sports and exercise psychology for the next three years and some of the lecturers are younger than me never mind my fellow students.

Sports psychology is something that has interested me for a long time but there is a big difference between having an interest in a subject and committing yourself to finding out so much more over a long period of time. When I started playing there were, of course, no sports psychologists. Now each of the 18 first-class counties employ one even if it is usually on a part-time basis. Back then, asking for help with the mental side of your game was undoubtedly perceived as a sign of weakness. I look back to the early period of my career and can think of a lot of extraordinarily talented cricketers who would have been even better had there been someone to confide in when they felt low or depressed.

I would see guys frying their brain over-thinking when things weren't going well when all they needed to do was strip it right back and simplify things as much as possible. I know. I was one of them. There were also players, of course, who can work things out for themselves but many more who could not. The best sports psychologists I worked with kept things simple. When I spoke to them I wasn't interested in theories. I just wanted to know what they could do to make me mentally stronger and what I needed to do to find the answers I needed.

I will give you an example. One of the things we learn on the degree course is a self-determination theory about what motivates people which is centred around three parts. Autonomy: If I was a coach I would want to give my players a certain amount of power; Competence: Make sure they know what they are doing; Relatedness: They need to have the feeling of being part of something. Seeing how that can work in a team environment fascinates me, especially the bit about making people feel that they want to play for a cause.

That always motivated me when I played and on that subject I think I speak for the vast majority of cricketers and, indeed, professional sportsmen. We laud individual achievements in sport but for me what the team delivers has always meant more, whether I am part of it or watching from the sidelines as I do now, because I am fascinated by what motivates the individuals who make up the team collective.

I am fortunate to have an advantage over my fellow students because I have the first-hand experience of certain situations that we study. For instance, I know what it's like to play in front of 75,000 people and still perform at a high level. So that helps now as I study the subject, but if I do end up working as a sports psychologist I certainly won't be the old pro who bases the information he imparts largely on his own experiences. For me, there has to be some theory, some evidence behind what you tell people as well. Knowing how I reacted during my career in certain challenging situations isn't necessarily what the individual you are talking to needs to know, or indeed the team.

I have always been interested in what makes sportsmen tick. For me, you can have the best technique in the world but you're not going to fulfil yourself if you lack the confidence to perform. On the other hand, if you have got lots of self-belief it's amazing what you can achieve even if you're not as talented as some of your peers.

It is inevitable that people see a link between what I have suffered since 2011, when I was first diagnosed with depression, and my decision to study sports psychology. But, as I have explained, there is so much more to it for me.

I have so much newly-found respect for anyone studying for a degree, no matter their age or their subject. I do like learning but this is very much a means to an end for me, I'm quite clinical about it really. I'm certainly not there to enjoy the social side of university life. I went out with a few of the other students last Christmas but if you asked me where the students' union is on the campus at Chichester I'd have to ask someone first!

In terms of lectures and coursework I have to devote about 12 hours a week. I find it all very interesting but the pure learning part is not easy for me. I have to spend a lot of time reading and re-reading things before they sink in. Equally, I can spend ages writing a report or an essay before I'm satisfied with it and understanding statistical analysis is very hard too which is kind of ironic given that, for the previous 15 years, statistics played such a big part in my life! I think I can quickly pick up how certain theories can work while my own dissertation is based on mental toughness, and specifically whether you can make a 17-year-old as mentally strong as, say, a 26-year-old. Committing those thoughts to paper, now that's the difficult part for me.

The other students know who I am and what I have achieved in the game and they occasionally chat to me about my own experiences with Sussex and England. Mind you, the only time they have seen footage of me in action was the 2010 T20 World Cup Final and, specifically, my first over when Australia's Cameron White started crashing me around the Kensington Oval in Barbados. I just told them that was one of those moments when you wish you'd had a great final and a crap tournament rather than the other way around.

If I do get a degree, working full-time in sports psychology is an obvious ambition and it doesn't have to be in cricket. I'd love the opportunity to work in other sports. Every time I watch sport now I find myself trying to analyse how individuals react to certain situations. It fascinates me. I played with a lot of cricketers I would describe as being mentally strong. I never thought 'I wish I was like that' but I did quietly admire guys like Paul Collingwood, who embraced every aspect of his profession, and Andrew Strauss, who was amazingly talented of course but who could also accept that on certain days his opponent would be better than him. He could quickly move on whereas I found that a lot tougher.

When I retired coaching opportunities weren't something I actively sought, but in the autumn of 2015 Nick Creed, who I played junior cricket with for Sussex all those years ago, approached me through Keith Greenfield, Sussex's recently-appointed director of cricket, about working at Hurstpierpoint College, where Nick is in charge of the cricket department. I accepted the position after we met and so on several afternoons in the winter of 2015/16 you'd have found me on the playing fields at the college, coaching football and, on occasion, even refereeing a match before my focus switched to looking after the cricket in the spring of 2016.

I'm not a teacher, I'm a coach and I really enjoy helping the youngsters to get better. I try to steer away from old-school coaching methods where the emphasis is on drilling down technique. I like challenging the kids to see what they can do, rather than telling them what I think they should be doing. It's the same with my work with the Sussex under-17s age group squad. I will be coaching them for the first time in 2016 after accepting an invitation from Keith Greenfield. We play four three-day and four one-day games as well as squad training sessions and I am looking forward to putting some of my theories into practice to what I hope is a responsive group of boys.

When I played representative junior cricket I often felt players held something back. You didn't want to play without fear because you didn't think it wouldn't impress the coaches who, first and foremost, were looking for youngsters who had mastered the basics of the game very well. I think it's different now. I'm looking for kids who can do something different, a certain skill they have that will make them stand out from the rest and catch the coach's eye when they get the opportunity to train with the professionals.

I like to challenge them. "Can you do something that no one has ever done on a cricket field before?" Cricket has evolved so much during the length of my career and certainly since the advent of T20 in 2003 when, suddenly, batsmen discovered they had to ditch the orthodox and try something different: ramp shots, scoops, whatever. All the time new shots are being invented and one day I am sure a bowler will be able to execute six different deliveries in an over to absolute perfection or come up with a wicket-taking ball that no one has bowled before. Hard to believe now, but when I made my one-day debut for Sussex hitting a six was almost a cause for celebration in itself.

As well as the Sussex under-17s and my commitments at Hurstpierpoint College I am also doing some coaching with Middleton, a Sussex League club whose captain is a former team-mate of mine, Sean Heather. I've already told him there's no chance of me playing, even in a crisis. As I mentioned, I've only got one bat left and no kit and I have no intention of buying any more. I was asked if I'd play T20 for Sussex if there was an emergency at Hove. Sorry, but the answer's the same. No thanks.

During my benefit year in 2014 I decided to give some of the proceeds to Mind, the charity which raises awareness of mental health, and I did some work with the media to promote the work they do. Entrenched views about mental illness, such as those espoused by Geoff Boycott when I left the World Cup in 2011, are still out there and the task of changing people's perceptions, particularly among the older generation, about mental health is something that will probably never end. The message I tried to stress was that you can be struggling mentally but are still able to perform. Of course, if you're not sleeping or your self-esteem is low, it will invariably overlap into your performance on the field but a diagnosis of depression is still something you can live with. Hopefully, the way people view mental illness is slowly changing and anything I can do to help promote Mind I will happily do in the future.

Tough as it was at the time for myself and, before me, Marcus Trescothick, the publicity our plight generated was very important in terms of raising awareness. But for every high-profile sufferer there are hundreds of people living quietly and stoically with mental illness, whether they are suffering or someone close to them is. Sometimes all they need is someone who understands to confide in. For me, the hardest thing about my mental illness was not admitting it but trying to understand why I was suffering. There's no doubt it was detrimental to me in the last four years of my career, as my record shows. The positive for me is that it has definitely made me a better, more rounded person. I am far more tolerant of others now than I was before and I understand why I experience certain feelings much better than I did before my diagnosis.

So how would I describe my mental health now? Well, I still have bad days but they are nowhere near as regular as they were two or three years ago. I can spot the signs so much better as well. Not sleeping well is the main trigger or periods when my mind is flooded with unhelpful thoughts.

I have always been a bit of a dreamer. When I was playing I'd imagine winning games for England and Sussex on my own. Now, it's more likely to involve being the sports psychologist for the New York Yankees and working with top athletes.

When I get my degree I want to be the best at my profession in the world, using all the experiences I've had in cricket and life in my new vocation. The problem with these dreams of mine is that if I have a knockback it can hit me very, very hard.

When I started to study for my degree the first mark I got was a fail. And because I have been living in this fantasy world for too long, dreaming of this meteoric rise to the top of my profession, I would catastrophise things instead of thinking in practical terms about what I needed to do to get my mark up. I know that by thinking like that I am setting myself up for a massive fall but sometimes it's hard to stop. For a few hours or a couple of days my world will come crashing down and I will regard myself as a failure. But slowly I have begun to realise that this wonderful utopian world doesn't exist, for me or for anyone really. So now I set myself smaller, more realistic and infinitely more achievable goals like being the best dad I can be.

I was asked recently where I saw myself in five years. As I have explained, a job as a sports psychologist would be fantastic and I don't think it's an unrealistic goal but I still have a huge passion for cricket and for coaching the game. I hope knowing about sport psychology will help me become a good coach and enable me to look at things with a slightly different perspective. Who knows, I might be Sussex coach one day. I think I'd have a lot to offer. I never used to worry that I would never be a professional cricketer and it's the same now. I will have a worthwhile career whether it's in my chosen field or something else. And over the last four or five years I have learned not to worry too much about what the future holds. It will work itself out.

As I was putting the finishing touches to this book the 2016 season was about to get underway although I certainly didn't feel any pangs of jealousy as the Sussex boys donned bobble hats and extra layers to play pre-season friendlies in the early spring chill and prepare for the arduous six-month grind of the county summer. I definitely don't miss the training that is involved these days. I still like going to the gym but now I don't have to spend hours on the treadmill or doing those dreaded leg strengthening exercises that I used to hate. I like to keep fit and I play the odd game of five-a-side football but I don't feel I have a massive void to fill with something else now cricket has gone. I will go to Hove to watch a few Sussex games but I'll be looking at things from a slightly different perspective. Why is that player doing that? What about his body language? How will the batsman or bowler react to a high-pressure situation? For me that is far more interesting than mere bat on ball.

I feel very fortunate to have had the career I had and to have played during the start of the T20 era. Would I have played for England if T20 hadn't been invented? Possibly not, there is no doubt that it was the format of the game I felt most comfortable with, certainly at international level. The last few years of my career were a bit of a grind but I can still look back on certain games when I was completely contented. Perhaps the happiest I felt wasn't the World Cup Final in 2010 when we beat Australia but a few weeks earlier in the tournament in a qualifying group game against Pakistan.

My first over went for 12 runs and Paul Collingwood immediately took me out of the attack. I remember retreating to the outfield and having this amazing clarity of thought. "Right, that's it. When I get the ball again I am going to get it right. No more excuses. I am going to perform." I can't remember feeling more motivated on a cricket field than I did at that point. Graeme Swann took a wicket and I came back on and bowled my last three overs for seven runs and picked up two wickets. I'm not sure people who have followed my career would necessarily think of that bowling spell as a career highlight. It might not even get in their top ten but knowing that I had to perform after that poor first over and then delivering my skills in the way I did still makes me feel proud even now, six years or more later. I thought I was going to be dropped after bowling just one over in the tournament proper. Remember, we left some pretty good players out of that team including James Anderson so getting into the team in the first place was not easy. Sometimes, though, it's not about skill. It can be about having that sheer bloody-mindedness to perform at your best. When I had that I invariably found that the rest took care of itself – I got runs or took wickets or bowled economically under pressure.

If I look back on that game as a career high then the lowest point for me happened just over a year later when I retreated from the outfield at Hove, during a T20 match against Middlesex, in a state of panic. I said afterwards that I felt I was in danger. To this day I don't know what 'danger' represented, I just knew I could not be on that field for a moment longer. That night I thought my career was over. I didn't think I'd be able to carry on.

Fortunately, and thanks to the unstinting support of so many people who have been part of my journey so far, I was able to play again. I was able to come to terms with mental illness and to live with it. I didn't have the same success in the last four years of my career and when I did call it a day I knew it was the right decision. But now the next chapter of my life is underway and I feel just as excited and enthused about what lies ahead as I did on the first day I walked into the County Ground at Hove, with my chaperone James Kirtley alongside me, to begin my life as a professional cricketer.

14

Dealing with depression

by Karin Yardy

IT has been eight years now since Mike, my husband, first started to experience depression. There have been some very difficult episodes for both of us since then but as I sit here, in the spring of 2016, I'm hopeful that perhaps the very worst is thankfully behind us. Mike hasn't needed to see a therapist since June 2015 and I'm convinced that his decision to retire from cricket, which he announced a month later before playing his final game for Sussex in September 2015, is a big factor in his improvement. It has certainly made our home life a lot better having him around much more. The kids and I adore him – as we always have – and he has now got a big space in his life which was taken up by cricket for 16 years that he can devote to his new path as a student and, of course, his family.

The improvements in his condition are such that on his last visit to his therapist she told Mike that there was light at the end of the tunnel, that he is getting better. Of course it would be fantastic if he were to be cured totally but we both know that is unlikely to happen. She didn't mean that he wouldn't suffer anymore, rather that he will continue to deal with it better and that every time he has bad days in the future it will take less time for him to come out of it and be fine again. But we know that it will always be there so we carry on taking each day as it comes, thankful that the bad days are now fewer and farther between than they were in the past. I hope so, because to see Mike suffer as he has done has just been so heart-breaking for me as his wife.

I'll be honest. At times there have been days, certainly when Mike first started to suffer, when I was not great at dealing with it. Normally, I will know the moment I wake up in the morning if Mike is in a bad place. He will have been up and down the stairs during the night because he can't sleep – bouts of insomnia are linked to the type of depression he suffers from. I will start talking to him – just normal stuff like who is dropping the kids off to school – and I will sense there is this cloud over him and that I will just have to gather the children up, go out for a few hours and let Mike rest and de-stress. Over the years, if he is suffering for any length of time, I have learned to take little steps to try and bring him back to normality. For instance, after a couple of days in bed, we will coax him out of the house just to go for a walk or take the children to the park or the beach.

I try to keep everything as normal as possible for our three kids – Syenna, Raffy and Marley. They don't know about what their dad suffers from at the moment, but one day we will talk to them about it. Our eldest, Syenna, is quite switched on and I guess in a couple of years we will have that conversation with her. For now, though, they are just happy that their daddy is around a lot more than he was to take them to the swings and do the things dads do with their children.

When Mike is in what I call one of his black holes he will over-analyse everything and make this massive leap forward in terms of how he imagines certain situations will pan out. When he first started to get depressed in 2008 this would regularly have been something to do with physical fitness. He would have found an exercise he wanted to do at the gym to improve his strength or general condition that he would literally do day in, day out for weeks on end. It would become his sole focus. Another instance of him concentrating on one thing to the detriment of pretty much everything else would be his diet. He would discover something that he thought would help and latch onto that. Mike would insist that all this made him a better cricketer because by focussing on things like conditioning and nutrition so intensely it made him fitter and therefore improved him as a player. I would just sigh and think 'not another thing'.

I guess we are fortunate in a way that Mike's illness doesn't make him feel like harming himself. Even during his worst moments, I have never thought he would hurt himself. There have been a couple of occasions when I have wondered whether it was better to stay at home with him but that's just to keep him company, not because I thought he would do something untoward.

I must admit I was absolutely delighted when Mike told me a few weeks into the 2015 season that he was going to retire. He had suffered a couple of bad episodes at the start of the season, ironically one in the same Southampton hotel where he had suffered badly in 2010 when he had to come home early from England's one-day series against Pakistan.

When he announced his retirement in 2015 he had actually been playing well, although by then he was also studying for his university course and I was concerned, naturally, that he might be taking on too much. He came back from Sussex's pre-season tour to Dubai pretty relaxed but a couple of days into the first Championship match against Hampshire he came home and the following morning told me of his intention to give up cricket. My first reaction was "Oh my God! He's actually done it!" There had been many occasions before then, as mental illness started to take hold, when he spoke about giving up the game. So for me there was a massive sense of relief that he had finally decided to do so but also a lot of sadness, because I know how much the game has meant to him for the past 15 years. It sounds odd and I will explain what I mean later, but the symptoms of his depression actually drove him on to become the very best player he could, to make the utmost out of the talent he had. In the end, though, he'd had enough.

Now, post-cricket, things are very different at home. He still suffers from peaks and troughs in his moods because doing exams and coursework can be stressful. I studied French at university and know that it can be difficult coping with the workload at times, but he attends his lectures, sees his tutors or does his sports coaching at Hurstpierpoint College during the day and then comes home in the evening and, unless West Ham are on TV, his focus is on the family and spending time with me and the kids, which is lovely.

There were many periods during his career when he didn't seem to be able to relax at all and during that time we hardly did anything between periods when he was playing cricket. If there was a party or something we'd been invited to he wouldn't want to go because he wanted to be as well prepared as he could be for his next cricket match, whether it was a game against a university team for Sussex or England versus Australia. In the end I accepted that although I didn't like it at the time.

I know that since Mike packed up cricket I am so much happier and I think Mike is as well. He is always concerned that the illness will rear its ugly head to the extent it did during the really bad episodes but I don't think it will because he is so much more relaxed now. He is the Yards I met in 2003, he's so chilled out. And of course not playing cricket has opened up so much time in his life for other stuff.

I was in my final year at Aston University when we first met in the students' union bar. He was visiting a friend and having a few drinks. Actually, he'd had a lot to drink! But we got talking and I remember asking him what he did. His response was: "Oh, I play a bit of cricket." Nothing more than that. But I was intrigued and the next day a friend and I searched him on the internet. There wasn't much about Mike back then but I knew it was him when I saw his picture and read that he was a young professional at Sussex. It made no difference to me. I knew absolutely nothing about cricket. My family aren't into the game at all so it wasn't a sport I was interested in really.

Like Mike, I was born near the coast in Margate, Kent. Our family then lived in Herne Bay for 14 years before we moved to Hong Kong for a few years, because of my father Barrie's work, which we loved. I went to school there and when I came back I headed straight off to university to study French. My mum is French which is where the unusual spelling of my name originates. It's a constant bugbear of mine when people mis-spell it! They settled in France in 1999 and their home has been a refuge for me and the children on many occasions when Mike has been away playing cricket for England.

I promised my parents I wouldn't get a boyfriend in my final year at university so I could concentrate on my exams. We met in January so I nearly got through and fortunately the distraction didn't prevent me from achieving my degree. After that first meeting Mike and I kept in touch by phone but I didn't see him again for four or five weeks. Then, he came up to Birmingham but had only been there one day when he got a call from Peter Moores, who was Sussex coach at the time, telling him he had to go and play a game somewhere. So I got used to him being away because of cricket pretty early in our relationship.

I remember thinking he was just so incredibly relaxed as a person. We used to talk for hours about everything and anything, except cricket. He was interested in my degree because he hadn't gone to university and we just hit it off straight away. I felt totally comfortable with him, I never felt I had to put a front on when I was with Mike. With Mike, what you see is what you get and that's always been the case. Within three months of meeting we had moved in together.

When my university course finished I moved back to Herne Bay in June 2003 and my plan was to find a job in London and commute. I didn't really think about moving to Sussex at all then. It wasn't on the radar, even though Mike and I were going steady. I'd been looking solidly for a job for a couple of weeks with no luck when Mike suggested I come to Hove for a break and to see what was on offer work-wise down in Sussex. He was coming back from a match somewhere and picked me up, which was also the first time that he met my mum and dad.

He was living in a studio flat on the seafront – it was a typically horrible bachelor's pad – but I loved being by the seaside. There had been a big support network of friends when I had been at university so this was the first time I'd properly lived away from home. I remember sitting on the beach one sunny afternoon, thumbing through the graduate jobs section in the *Guardian* newspaper, thinking this was an amazing life. Then the next day Mike was off playing cricket somewhere which kind of took the gloss off things a bit!

We rented a few different places in Hove but he wanted to get away from there so we took a flat in Redhill for six months. At the time we had lots of friends who lived in London so it made sense as it was a lot easier to get up there to socialise, but eventually we realised that it was a bit daft being so far away from Hove, the place where we both worked, and we decided to buy a flat just up the road in Lancing.

Mike actually proposed to me by text message – he has never been one for grand romantic gestures! That was in 2004 and a couple of weeks later we went to London for the weekend to buy an engagement ring. I told him he had to ask my father's permission. I would never describe Mike as shy but he doesn't put himself out there so I don't suppose talking to Barrie about it was an easy conversation for him. In the end he just said, "I've asked Karin to marry me, I hope that's okay."

We got married in October 2005 and Mike had to get permission from Peter Moores, who'd just taken over as coach of the England Academy at Loughborough, to turn up late after he'd been picked to attend squad sessions up there. On our honeymoon I remember spending a whole morning on the beach near the hotel doing throw-downs while he batted the ball back with a tennis racquet or had some catching practice. That's love I suppose!

That Academy call-up was the first time he went away for any length of time and initially, when it was still just the two of us, it never bothered me. I was used to it because my father went all over the world with his business. They say you sometimes marry a person who is like your father and in that case it's definitely true. My mum Catherine had to become very independent when she was bringing up myself and my little sister Amy pretty much on her own and for a few years that was what happened to me.

It was when we started to have a family that the periods away became hard for both of us. Then it wasn't much fun. Before we had Syenna, I joined him in Barbados for a week at the end of the England A tour in 2006 and we had a fantastic time and I also went to New Zealand between the birth of Raffy and our third child Marley. If I have one regret, it's that I could have gone to a lot more places when Mike was in the England team and didn't, but I had always wanted to start a family fairly quickly and I was 25 when Syenna was born.

Mike was in Australia on another England training camp when I was heavily pregnant and he needed permission to come home for her birth. Syenna was due on 14 December, 2006 and he came back home six days earlier. I hated the thought that he might not have been around for her birth but in the end she wasn't born until Christmas Eve. Mike has been at the birth of all our children, although he only just made it for Raffy having driven like a maniac down the A23 from The Oval during Sussex's match against Surrey.

Syenna was five weeks old when Mike had to go to Bangladesh early in 2007. That was the first time I thought 'I don't like him going away.' He hated the separation too. Matt Prior came to pick him up so they could drive to the airport together to meet the rest of the team but Mike and I were in floods of tears on the doorstep. Before, we'd just got on with it but this was different. I decamped to France with Syenna to spend time with my parents but that was probably the first time I sensed something wasn't quite right with Mike. We had many conversations when he was in India when I would have to persuade him not to quit the tour, which he wanted to do.

In August 2008 Raffy was born and we moved to Australia for the winter when he was five weeks old. With a new-born and a two-year-old it was a very stressful time but we were looking forward to this exciting adventure with our young family although it turned out to be anything but.

The club Mike was playing for had sorted out the accommodation for us in a place called Lathlain and the house, to put it mildly, was a shit hole. I remember walking in, totally exhausted after the long flight, and wanting to turn around there and then and come home. It was an old, run-down, horrible property. We'd been there for a couple of weeks when my parents, who were in Australia doing their own grand tour, came to see us which was nice but it was still a tough time. I thought the cricket club would be similar to Sussex, a place where all the wives and girlfriends would meet to socialise during the matches, but Mike hardly played there.

That was when I noticed his OCD tendencies for the first time. As he has mentioned in an earlier chapter, I thought the house was perfectly safe but Mike did not. He hardly slept as a result of his anxiety and on New Year's Eve I remember he got up in the middle of the night and by next morning he'd decided we were going to move and had already been online to find us a place. As well as that episode Mike was going constantly to the gym. Obviously he had to keep fit but he was never out of the place for a few weeks. It had turned into an obsession.

Something was clearly not right but the thought that he might be depressed certainly didn't cross my mind. I would never have believed it even if a specialist had given him a spot diagnosis there and then. We didn't really talk about it but Mike was already starting to hide what he was suffering from really well anyway. I know now that he didn't want to burden me with it, especially as I had my hands full with two young children. I was in this bubble and sometimes it was just a case of getting through the day and the sleepless nights, but I subsequently found out that he was very scared that something was seriously wrong with him.

Mike isn't someone who wears his heart on his sleeve. He does so a bit more now but back then I can't imagine he would have even admitted to feeling depressed because he would have thought it was a sign of weakness. And in any event, I'm sure he didn't want to believe that it might be the case anyway.

Life in Perth did improve. We eventually found a babysitter so we could go out every Friday and our new place was much better for us, close to the beach and in an area where there was a lot more going on. The downside was that Mike had to travel a bit further to train at the club but from the family's point of view we started to enjoy the outdoor Australian lifestyle. Then his best friend, John McSweeney, came out with his girlfriend for a couple of weeks for a holiday and we had a brilliant time together. Mike seemed a lot less stressed when John was there but when they returned his mood went a bit flat again. We had about a month left then but my dad had been in touch about a big family reunion back in the UK which I really wanted to attend so we came back a couple of weeks early. I think we were both glad to get home.

At that stage Mike's condition was still something that was in the background and I wasn't affected directly that much. But Mike would begin to have more and more days when he would feel low and I would get angry and resentful. 'Just fucking get out of bed and do something,' was, I'm ashamed to say now, my response on more than one occasion. To my mind, he had to crack on.

There were days when I would stomp around downstairs feeling very pissed off. I was trying to juggle my own career with bringing up two young kids and thinking 'I need him to come out of this soon.' It never lasted that long but it still makes me shudder now to think about my lack of understanding towards him, simply because I didn't know what was wrong. I was so ignorant of what was happening to Mike. My reaction, which I guess a lot of people in the same situation would have had they encountered the same scenario in their life, was to insist that he snaps out of it. Whatever 'it' was. We still didn't really know.

Then things changed. Mike had gone off to play for England in a one-day series against Pakistan in late August 2010. Initially it went well. He won a man of the match award for the first time but, as the series progressed, the phone calls became more frantic, his mood more anxious. I was scared so God knows how he felt but when we spoke practical Karin always kicked in. I reassured him it was all fine and that the series would soon be over and he could come home to his family and chill out.

On the morning he rang me from Southampton in tears I told him he had to go and speak to Andy Flower, the England coach, and tell him he couldn't play. That must have been a very hard conversation for Mike to have. I'm not sure I could have done it.

He felt better being back at home but then the doubts began to bubble up to the surface. Earlier that year Mike had been part of the T20 World Cup winning team and was one of the best players in that format in the country. I thought that the England management would handle his situation sympathetically going forward, which they did, but he went into a sort of panic mode. He was convinced that was the end of his international career and for the first time he openly talked about giving up cricket for good, convinced, as he was back then, that it was the game – and more specifically the pressures of playing for England – that were the root cause of his problems.

A few weeks later, when we were finally told that Mike had depression, it was 100 times scarier because suddenly it was real and something we were going to have to get used to dealing with. But there was also a sense of relief for both of us because he knew what it was now and could deal with it, whether that be sessions with therapists or going on medication.

At the time we were living in Lancing but we wanted to move back to Brighton because nearly all our friends, our social circle and our support network was there. But when Mike first mentioned giving up cricket hard-headed practical Karin soon kicked that idea into touch. We'd just signed our mortgage papers on a new house and if he'd gone public and announced his retirement and the reasons for it we would have surely lost the mortgage, even though Mike had saved his England appearance money towards a deposit. The credit crunch was on at that time and banks and lenders were finding any excuse not to lend money to people, probably even England cricketers. I was worried that we'd be stuck in our old house and back to square one.

Of course had I known what he was going through, and how awful it was, I would never have reacted like that. In his early sessions with the therapist Mike was told not to make big decisions when he was in a bad place and that is something that has stuck with him ever since. If he makes what I think is a rash judgement I have learned to accept it at the time knowing that a few days later, when he is feeling better, he will invariably change his mind. The only time he didn't was when he finally decided to retire in 2015 and by then I was happy to go along with that.

Now it was no longer a secret I tried to get Mike to talk more about his feelings but he continued to hide it well. There would be many occasions over the next few months and years when I thought he was absolutely fine and then a couple of hours later I'd get a call from Mark Robinson, the Sussex coach, from the ground to say he would have to come home. That made me feel a bit of a failure as a wife to be honest, not being able to spot that he was having a bad day. Eventually, when I began to recognise the signs more clearly, I would always insist that he stayed at home to rest and I would have to ring Mark and tell him he wasn't coming to cricket.

Mike was due to go to New Zealand and Australia during the winter of 2010/11. It was going to be a long time away from home, although I was due to fly to New Zealand to be with him for a few weeks before Christmas. I should probably have been concerned but I wasn't because I knew that now he had a good support network with him in terms of the England team management, who were obviously aware that he could have black moods after what had gone on in Southampton. He was really excited about the trip and when I flew out we had a great time. He then went to Australia to play in the one-day series and produced some of his best performances in 50-over cricket for England and was certainly in contention to play in the World Cup in India and Sri Lanka.

But it all started again when he came home for a few days before flying off to India for the start of the tournament in

February 2011. In hindsight, it was a big mistake for him to come home although at the time myself and the children all wanted Mike back, even if it was only for a while, because he would soon be off again and might not be returning for more than a month. I still have photos of those few days, of Mike sprawled across the sofa with the kids milling around him. He hardly moved from the couch the whole time. He clearly didn't want to leave us again but he just got on with it.

When he got out to the World Cup we talked every day and sometimes Skyped, although that was difficult because the children would see their dad on a computer screen and couldn't understand why he was so far away which was upsetting for them. Knowing how hard it had been for him to leave us to go on the tour I expected to have to reassure him that everything would be fine once he got into a familiar routine of playing and practising but, as I subsequently learned, there wasn't anything I could say at that time which would have made him feel better about his cricket or anything. Subsequently, I learned to say nothing in those situations and instead I always made sure we went out to dinner or had a change of scene so we could talk about something else.

During the World Cup, he would constantly be questioning himself in our conversations and told me he didn't feel he was worthy of playing for his country. He said that he had heard snippets of conversations around the camp and was worried he was going to be left out of the team. This used to happen a lot when he was with England but it was definitely worse, I felt, during that tournament.

When he rung me to say he was flying back from the World Cup in March 2011 I must admit I had expected the call. I still remember what he told me: "I'm coming home tomorrow, I'm not right. I'm going to come out and say I am having treatment for depression. I have nothing to be ashamed of." I was just relieved that he would be back home in a day or so, with his family, so he could relax, get treatment and get better. I know Mike has since said that publicly admitting the reason why he was coming home early from the World Cup might have been a mistake but at the time, in those minutes after he told me, I didn't give it a second thought. I was quite glad for him and us.

But then the following day, when he was due to fly into Heathrow where I would pick him up, two things happened. First I got a phone call from Hugh Morris, the ECB's chief executive, to say that both he and the ECB's media manager Andrew Walpole would be there to greet him as well. I remember coming off the phone thinking why would he need a welcoming party?

Then I got a call from a friend who worked in London to tell me that I was on the back page of that day's *Evening Standard*. The story said that Mike had admitted he was coming home to be treated for depression, which was along the lines of the statement issued by the ECB. My reaction was that they had taken a fairly straightforward statement and blown the whole thing out of proportion but then I went online to read the report and was horrified. A journalist had gone onto my Facebook page and lifted a picture of me and the children to use with the article. If that wasn't bad enough, they had used a quote of mine which I'd written on a status update. It was the most ridiculous thing. Raffy had walked out of the house to visit his best friend two doors up the street wearing Syenna's tutu and ballet shoes! He was only three at the time, bless him. I wrote: 'Typical, Mike goes away and the house goes to pot – Raff's outside wearing his sister's tutu!' And from that inoffensive comment they had turned it into a story about the stresses that families are under when England cricketers go on tour. I was more concerned that they had used a picture of the children without my permission. They claimed they had been trying to get hold of me but no journalist had ever spoken to me.

When I got to Heathrow I had a coffee with Hugh and Andrew. I was quite jovial and excited about the thought of seeing my husband again but their mood was totally different. They told me they were there to make sure that the press didn't button-hole Mike as he came out of the arrivals hall. In the past, when I'd gone to collect him after England trips, I had got used to the media being there but this time there was no one. I subsequently learned that the ECB had asked the media to respect my privacy and, apart from the *Evening Standard*, they did. He wasn't harassed and there were no reporters camped on the doorstep when we got home.

When I saw him come through the gate I knew why they had reason to be worried. He looked awful, it was as if he had been drugged. When we got home we went into lockdown for three or four days. Before meeting him practical Karin kicked in again when I texted all our family and friends, prior to the ECB's announcement, to say that Mike was coming home and why and that they should not worry. Was that hard for me to do? I'm not sure it was, even now. I think at the time I was on a bit of an emotional rollercoaster but my over-riding priority was protecting Mike.

In the event everyone was brilliant about what had happened. We had lots of positive messages from friends which definitely helped. What was more interesting was how many people were contacting us to say that either they or people close to them were also suffering from a form of depression including individuals we knew who we thought were absolutely fine. It was amazing. We received literally hundreds of letters from total strangers, which I have still got, expressing support for Mike, saying he was not alone and wishing him good luck for the future. Those letters helped me hugely at the time.

Gradually we have learned what the signs are when Mike feels bad and what he – and the rest of us – can do to deal with it. In order for him to feel better about himself when he gets himself in a low place he needs to feel busy. His life is about finding that balance between resting when he is ill and giving himself time, when he does get better, to go back to work – which for the last 16 years has been cricket – and resume that and everyday life in general. If he goes back too early he can be at risk of a relapse.

But it wasn't until 2014, when he negotiated what was his final contract with Sussex, that he realised that if he delayed his return to the team then he was at the risk of losing his livelihood. It was a classic catch-22 situation.

A few weeks after his return from the World Cup Mike was back playing for Sussex. Was it too early given he subsequently had a bad episode during a T20 game against Middlesex? Probably, but if he hadn't gone back he would just have been miserable at home. I was at Hove watching the Middlesex game and enjoying a glass of wine. Kate Green, who was working for the PCA at the time and who helped Mike a lot in those first few months after his diagnosis, came to sit beside me and asked how he was. I told her that he was feeling really good. Then literally a moment or two later Mark Robinson phoned to ask me to come to the dressing room to collect him because he'd walked off the field in tears and needed to go home.

By then Mike was getting treatment and seeing therapists but as the weeks and months went by I found myself wanting to find out more about depression. I looked online a lot but I felt that was a total waste of time because most of the stuff you read is so scary and frightening. If you type the word depression into a search engine all this stuff comes up about suicide.

At the time I didn't know how to deal with it. I went to a session with Mike, at the insistence of his therapist, but that didn't help. The only thing that did was reading a book that had been sent to Mike by Steve Harmison, his former England team-mate. I read the first couple of chapters and it hit home instantly. Basically, it said that you just have to ride with it. It talked about how everyone's reasons for becoming depressed are different, that you can't control it, that treatment is different – there simply is not a one size fits all approach. I gave the book to my mum and one of my friends because I knew it would also stop them pre-judging what mental illness is and help them to understand that treatment is a question of time and a case of working out what works for each individual sufferer.

By far the scariest time for me was the incident at the end of 2012 when Mike thought he had hurt someone in Brighton with a couple of his friends. Mike likes a night out now and again but alcohol makes him feel terrible the next day so he knows his limits. I was pregnant with Marley at the time and I remember coming down in the middle of the night to find him asleep on the kitchen floor so I left him to it, figuring he must have had a few too many. The next morning, he was merely worried that he had said some daft things to his friends the previous evening. It was a few weeks later before he started having these strong feelings that he had killed someone. I kept saying that if he had the police would have been round to arrest him by now. It was one of the first times when he didn't hide his feelings very well because it was simply too big a deal. For weeks he couldn't get this thought out of his head and for the first time since his diagnosis I felt lost, that I genuinely couldn't help him. Just before Marley was born I remember having lunch and discussing what had happened with my mum in Brighton and bursting into tears, just as Mike walked into the restaurant to join us.

All I could do was advise him to go and see his therapist. He was taking medication, but, not for the first time, I seriously thought 'what's the point of taking pills when you're still getting depressed or feeling that you've harmed someone?' Eventually, after another session with a therapist who convinced him that he was imagining this scenario, those feelings went away and we could get back to something approaching normality but I know how very scared Mike was at the time.

Mike was verbally offered a new contract by Sussex during the 2013 season, but they didn't follow it up with anything formal for several months and we both began to fret. At that stage he wanted to carry on playing. He'd given up the captaincy and was looking forward to a few years trying to help the team win more trophies. Still, we heard nothing from the club until the beginning of 2014 when Mark Robinson and Paul Khoury, Sussex's physiotherapist, came round to the house to see us both. Normally I never got involved with Mike's contract discussions but this time they insisted I was present.

The club wanted to put things in place purely for Mike's well-being. It felt to me like an intervention but I could understand their point of view and I know it was done with the best of intentions for him. Mike told them if they were concerned that he might miss games because of his illness to change his contract so he was paid a basic salary and then appearance money on top of that, which is what happened. They also reassured me that if Mike didn't feel right that there was always someone at the club we could get in touch with. But that certainly brought home to us that this was a bigger beast we were having to deal with and was something that could directly impact on our future livelihood.

When Mike decided to retire it was upsetting for both of us. But I thought it had to happen and, deep down, I know that Mike knew the time was right. After he had given up the Sussex captaincy in 2012 and started thinking about his future I told him that as far as I was concerned he could carry on playing cricket for as long as he wanted, but what had to stop was the periods when he was physically at home but mentally somewhere else. That's always what I struggled to cope with. How being totally immersed in cricket and his form affected our home and family life – that he was present, but not present. That's what it had been like for nearly ten years. Thoughts about the game were never far away for Mike.

After his diagnosis of depression, by his own admission he was drained of confidence on a cricket field and it became hard for him to get that desire back. When he decided to retire I suggested to him that he play those final few months of his career just for the simple pleasure of it. And when he scored those two centuries against Somerset and Yorkshire I thought he was. But then he told me why he was doing so well. Sussex were in a relegation battle, trying to avoid going into the second division of the County Championship, and he was focussed and motivated on making sure that didn't happen. That was so typical of Mike. The team always came first. I'm sure he would have preferred Sussex stayed up than going out in a blaze of glory himself.

When Sussex were playing Yorkshire in his penultimate game at Hove I was having a cup of tea at home with one of my friends and I checked the score on my phone to see that he was 50 not out. We carried on chatting away and the next time I looked he was on 93! So I hauled the kids into the car and sped down to the ground as quickly as I could. As always, Sam, the lovely gateman at the County Ground, wanted to have a chat but for once I had to tell him I couldn't stop. When he got to his hundred I was standing with Zac Toumazi, the chief executive, and Sussex chairman Jim May in floods of tears before being brought back to reality. The kids were starting to get cold and wanted to go home! So much for savouring the occasion.

It was the same for his last home match against Yorkshire. I was with the former Sussex bowler Ed Giddins. I was doing some work with his company and we arranged to have a meeting in the Players Club at the County Ground. When Mike got to his hundred and everyone in the ground gave him a fantastic standing ovation I was standing in front of Ed who was merrily taking pictures of the celebrations without an inkling that I was in floods of tears again. On his last day as a player at Hove I couldn't stop crying again. This time James Kirtley, who had known Mike for all of his Sussex career, was with the children and I at the bottom of the steps leading up to the players' dressing room.

The kids ran onto the outfield as he walked off to another standing ovation and he scooped Marley up in his arms while

Syenna and Raffy walked alongside him. The children then went into the dressing room while Mike cleared out his locker and said his goodbyes to some of the backroom staff for the last time. A couple of days later we were sitting at home reflecting on what we had both been through over the last few years and this time we were both in tears. I still get emotional now thinking about those last few days of his career and how it ended so perfectly for him.

We have been on an incredible journey and although I would not wish what Mike had to go through on anyone I know it has made us stronger as a couple. We have been very fortunate that throughout Mike's illness he has had a brilliant support network. The club, the PCA and in particular Mark Robinson and Keith Greenfield at Sussex have always been on the end of a phone. We feel so fortunate in that regard because I know there are thousands of people out there who don't have that knowledge that there is always someone they can talk to. They have to suffer the effects of this horrible illness, which can strike anyone at any time, alone. We have had some tough times but I can't begin to understand how hard it must be for anyone having to live with mental illness to do so alone.

When Mike was particularly bad and I felt I needed support I sometimes thought I couldn't speak to anyone because I was scared of the repercussions for Mike – that he might not get another contract because he kept missing the odd game. I guess it would have been the same had Mike worked in an office or something. In that scenario, I would never have been able to pick up the phone and say he's not coming in today because he's depressed. Since his diagnosis, so many people have spoken to us about their own personal experiences. What we went through was horrible but I have learned that you can't relate your own situation to anyone else's where depression is concerned. Sometimes people want reassurance, especially if they or their loved one has just been diagnosed. I just advise them to go and speak to a doctor or a specialist and try not to self-diagnose.

Ideally, one day in the future, there will be the same support networks for sufferers of mental illness as there are for those living with physical illnesses. Wouldn't it be great, for instance, if there were people who could help families who have to deal with depression and mental health issues. That's why Mike was proud to promote the work of the mental health charity Mind and never turns down the opportunity to talk about what he has gone through so he can raise awareness of something that affects one in four of us. We both hope that this book helps to do that as well.

As bad as he was, especially when that OCD stuff kicked in and he suffered that bad episode at the end of 2012, there is no doubt that it did help focus his mind during his career. Because he didn't have the natural talent of a lot of players, being on the edge a bit did drive him on and it definitely made him a better cricketer.

I don't think anyone can understand mental illness unless you have been through it. It's the same for anyone suffering from a serious physical illness, how much pain that person is going through. You will never really know unless it's happening to you. Mike's suffering has certainly made me a lot more open-minded. Before, I was probably one of those people who would go to work after a bad night because the kids were playing up and tell everyone I was depressed. I'm certainly a lot more careful with my words now. The word 'depressed' doesn't do justice to the black hole sufferers can find themselves in.

We're just so thankful that Mike is doing so much better now but I don't imagine I will ever be able to say he is cured. What we have learned over the years is how to deal with it better and on a day to day basis that makes a big difference. We have been through a horrible experience but in a lot of ways we are truly blessed. We have a lot to be thankful for and I hope a happy and healthy future lies ahead of us as a family. I now understand why the therapist told us that there would be light at the end of the tunnel.